THE ROOTS OF HALLOWEEN

LUKE EASTWOOD

The History Press Ireland

In memory of Hugh Brennan and John Wyse-Jackson.

First published 2021

The History Press
97 St George's Place, Cheltenham,
Gloucestershire, GL50 3QB
www.thehistorypress.co.uk
© Luke Eastwood, 2021

Dead tree illustration by Jazella from Pixabay
Moon illustration by Arek Socha from Pixabay

British Library Cataloguing in Publication Data.
A catalogue record for this book is available from the British Library.

ISBN 978 0 7509 9800 0

Typesetting and origination by Typo•glyphix
Printed in Great Britain

Trees for Life

From the moment we are born we begin slowly dying.

Live, live your life and shine brightly;

For when your candle has run down and spluttered out,

There is no going back, only the next step – into the unknown.

Contents

Acknowledgements

I'd like to thank Friends of *Tlachtga*, Joe Conlon and the owners of the Hill of Ward for reviving celebrations at *Tlachtga* (The Hill of Ward). Thank you to Gemma McGowan for organising ceremonies at the hill over many years, and for her help and advice in finishing this book. Many thanks to Michelle Alú for her thesis on *Tlachtga* and the use of quotations from Máiréad Bryd and Gemma McGowan. Many thanks to John Gilroy for his seminal book on *Tlachtga*, which inspired me to build on his research to create this book. I'd also like to thank Con Connor for showing me the original Druids' well, near *Tlachtga*, many years ago. Thank you to Billy Mag Fhionn for the use of excerpts from *Blood Rite: The Feast of St Martin in Ireland* and to Joe McGowan for use of extracts from *Echoes of a Savage Land*. Thanks to Treasa Kerrigan for assistance with the archaeological aspects of *Tlachtga* and for extra proof-reading! Thanks to Dr. Karen Ward for corrections and to Searles O'Dubhain for assistance with the cosmology. Thanks to *Duchas* for the use of extracts from the Schools' Collection and to Dr Stephen Davis of University College Dublin (UCD) for the use of archaeology reports. Thank you to Elena Danaan for the wonderful illustrations and to Del Richardson for the proofreading (and the best bread in Ireland). Thanks to Cyril Harrington for the *History Ireland* magazine, which proved very useful. A big thank you to Rachel and Micheline Scoazec for their testimony on Breton customs. Thank you to Morgan Daimler for the preface, kindly written at short notice. Thanks, as ever, to my partner, friends and family for their continual support and to my comissioning editor, Nicola Guy, and project editor, Ele Craker, for helping bring this book to fruition so quickly.

Preface

In the last twenty years *Samhain* had seen a surge in popularity in popular culture, showing up in references on well-known television shows, albeit usually mispronounced, and even personified by named characters. It has also remained one of the most well-loved holidays among various pagan followers and witches who embrace the ideas of *Samhain* as the start of a new year and as the so-called season of the witch. And yet in the middle of all of this renewed attention and excitement for the pagan holiday that represents the roots of the modern Halloween, those very roots are often overlooked or ignored. Material written about *Samhain* often focuses on wider, cross-cultural sources and on the more recent folk traditions and beliefs that were woven together into the holiday that we recognise today. This cross-cultural view has its place and value but sadly overlooks or minimises the most significant history of *Samhain*, which is found in Ireland.

Samhain is, as the language of its name should imply, at heart a holiday that comes from Ireland and is embedded intrinsically in its mythology. While most books may offer a bare few sentences about *Tlachtga*, if that much, the Hill of Ward is undeniably at the centre of *Samhain*'s history and story. It is essential to acknowledge and discuss this place and its mythology if one wants to really understand what *Samhain* is. The figures of *Tlachtga* and her father *Mug Roith* loom large over both the hill and the history of the holiday, yet too often go unacknowledged in the wider

Halloween narrative. We lose so many layers of richness when we forget these names and this place. There are not, to be sure, any clear answers to be found but the layers of story that we can uncover, and which Luke Eastwood has laid out so eloquently here, help us to see and understand the shape of the oldest iterations of the holiday and the main figures behind those stories.

As modern paganism has gained ground and strength, it has created its own understanding of what *Samhain* is and was, with an edited version of the history and little to no acknowledgement of the mythology that stretches back over millennia. This newer view takes a wider approach but in doing so misses much of the beauty and nuance found by studying the distinctly Irish roots of the holy day. To truly understand what *Samhain* is we must look beyond the surface of the meaning of the word and the simple division of the year into summer and winter and dig into the stories, archaeology and oldest practices, as well as the way those evolved over the centuries into the folk beliefs and practices found throughout the years. When we do, we find Neolithic monuments aligned to *Samhain*, a complex discussion of timing based on shifting calendar dates, and a wide range of folk practices that include both protection and divination. And behind it all, inextricably linked to each aspect, is the belief that the Otherworld is opened into the human world at this time. This too is an aspect of the holiday that is poorly understood these days but which is vital to understanding the deeper nature of *Samhain*; ultimately, it is impossible to separate the interaction with the Otherworld that occurs at this time with the celebration of the time itself. By taking this more holistic view that includes all of these diverse aspects, a deeper, fuller understanding of this significant holy day can be gained and incorporated into modern celebrations. It is honestly surprising that no one has previously made an attempt to lay out the Irish history of

Samhain in a full book for a pagan audience, as it is so much needed, making this text essential.

This holiday, this shift from summer to winter, has been acknowledged across time and was noted as one of ancient Ireland's most significant yearly events. It has regained some of this prestige today, having seen an amazing revival in the twenty-first century. It began with pagan celebrations on *Tlachtga*, which in recent memory became the *Samhain* Festival of Fire and now the *Púca* Festival, all of which shared a common goal in different ways, seeking to honour this pivotal point and gather people together in celebration. *Samhain* isn't frozen in time, isn't just what it was millennia ago, nor just what it is today; rather it is the culmination of all the history, each story, and every celebration that has come before and happens now. It is a living belief and practice, born in Ireland, and spreading outwards like the branches of a tree.

Morgan Daimler, author of *A New Dictionary of Fairies and Pagan Portals: Gods and Goddesses of Ireland*

Introduction

I first visited *Tlachtga*, the ancient Druidic site now known as the Hill of Ward, in 2004 on Halloween (Hallowe'en) on my own and shortly after that with a small band of Druids. We visited the little-known and abandoned ancient well to the south, still called *An Tobar Druí* (the Druid's Well), during the sunset, before climbing the hill to the sacred site itself. I distinctly remember the difficulty of lighting a fire, in the dark, in a small skillet, due to the intense wind. From there we journeyed to Tara and finally to *Sliéve Na Cailleach* (Loughcrew) with the sacred flame, ignited at *Tlachtga*, not by river or horse (of former times) but by car, nonetheless re-enacting an ancient ritual of fire, reaching back into pre-recorded history.

Celebrations at *Tlachtga* (Hill of Ward) recommenced at Halloween/ *Samhain* 1999, led by locals from the small town of Athboy, Co. Meath. Pagan ceremonies at *Tlachtga* returned not long after, in 2000, after an absence of hundreds of years, not led by Druids of old but by two Wiccans, Janet Farrar and Gavin Bone, in a kind of theatrical performance, rather than a religious ritual. This was continued in an evolving form from 2008 onwards by Gemma McGowan, in conjunction with esoteric practitioners of various paths – with her hard work overcoming political fights, opposition and many other difficulties along the way.

In late October 2019 my partner and I drove for more than two hours to St Brendan's Well on the central north side of Valentia Island to collect the holy water from a site that pre-dates Christianity by centuries, if not millennia. We also found what appeared to be the only accessible rowan tree, on the north-east corner of the island, from which I took a small branch with nine bright red rowan berries on it. On the afternoon of Halloween, a few days later, we brought the water and berried branch to Athboy. In the stand of trees (Fairgreen Ringfort) in the town park, alone except for one enthusiastic but uninvited photographer, we used both the holy water, branch and smoke to bless the sacred fire that would be lit after sunset, in preparation for the ceremony on *Tlachtga* hill itself.

Why did we go to such trouble you may ask? A simple explanation is that *Mogh Ruith*, supposed father of *Tlachtga* (after whom the place is named), lived on Valentia Island and, according to mythology, used rowan to great magical effect. His name and that of his daughter, *Tlachtga*, are once again associated with the festival of *Samhain* – a long-forgotten Irish religious festival of great importance that is the direct ancestor of modern Halloween. What we did was a small part of a much larger celebration – a bit of craic to some and a deadly serious and solemn spiritual event to others. Either way, *Samhain* and *Tlachtga* have once more begun to emerge into the public consciousness in Ireland and far beyond.

The roots of the hugely popular Halloween and its cultural activities have been mostly forgotten and are completely unknown by most non-pagan people who participate in them. However, the story of *Tlachtga* is not lost – the pathway back into the past is long overgrown but still there, lying in the pages of dusty old books, the folk practices of the Irish (and their diaspora) and indeed, buried in the land itself. The purpose of this book is to bring to light that which has been hidden from all but perhaps currently a few thousand people, for many hundreds of years. This place (*Tlachtga*) and this festival (*Samhain*) is a vital part of Irish pre-Christian religious and social culture, one that has somehow survived the passing of time and religious intolerance. It has survived, albeit in a mutated form, to become Halloween, an annual celebration across the world – this is its story.

The author blessing the ceremonial fire at Fair Green Ringfort, at Athboy,
Co. Meath, Ireland.

CHAPTER 1

Irish Cosmology and the Otherworld

This may seem a strange place to start, considering this is a book primarily about *Samhain* (*Samhuinn* in Scotland and *Nos Galan Gaeaf* in Wales), the ancient form of today's Halloween. In truth, this is the only logical place to start, as the festival of *Samhain* can only be fully understood within the context of the pre-Christian cosmology and practices of the ancient Irish – what is referred to as Druidism or Druidry.

Druidry has been revived in recent centuries, from the early 1700s onwards, but this is a new form of Druidism, more correctly called Neo-Druidry, as it has no continuous link with the religion/spirituality of the original Druids. The arrival of Rome in Western Europe drove Druidism into the ground except in Ireland and Scotland, but even there it did not long survive the arrival of Christianity in the fifth century CE. By all estimates it had more or less died out by the eighth century and persisted only in social practices, folklore, stories and customs but not as a viable religion that anyone could practise openly.

Despite the erosion of Druidism, first by the Roman Empire and secondly by the Christian Church, much of the pre-Christian structure and practices of Western Europe (and Ireland particularly) survived in a thinly disguised or mutated form. The pre-Christian view of the world and universe (or cosmology, if we choose to use a fancy term) survived both in the written word and the folk practices of the Irish, Scottish, Welsh, Breton and (to some extent) English peoples. It is to Ireland that we must look for the most complete model of how the Druids understood the world around them and what ways they celebrated the important moments of their year.

The Irish year was divided into two halves – winter (*geimhreadh*) and summer (*samhradh*), with winter preceding summer. We see the same thing in Gaul, as demonstrated by the Coligny calendar, with three days to celebrate *Samionos* (*Samhain*) – TRINVX SAMO SINIV or 'the three nights of *Samonios*'. In the same way as the year, the day was divided into two halves, with the night (from sunset) preceding the daylight. The year itself was subdivided into eight parts of approximately six weeks, each marked by a festival. These eight festivals began at the Celtic New Year, which was *Samhain*, summer's end, which is considered the entry point into the dark part of the year. The eight points of note are (in order) *Samhain*, winter solstice, *Imbolc*, spring equinox, *Bealtaine*, summer solstice, *Lughnasadh* and autumn equinox.

The equinoxes and solstices are universal, they have been celebrated by humanity across the world for millennia but the four 'Celtic' festivals are unique to Western Europe, although there are somewhat similar traditions in many countries around the world. All eight of these pagan festivals have managed to survive in Europe in a mutated Christianised form, which has already been covered amply in many books, so I will not discuss them here – it is sufficient to say that the placing of Christmas, Easter, the beginning of spring, the beginning of summer, harvest festival and All Hallows' Day is no accident.

In Ireland and other countries around the world, there are ancient sites of the Neolithic period (late Stone Age) that are very obviously aligned to the equinoxes and solstices. In Ireland in particular there are some ancient examples that stretch back to 4,000–3,000 BCE, with some, such as *Slíeve na Cailleach* showing evidence of much earlier constructions, that are now completely buried and invisible to the naked eye. Ancient sites in Ireland are also associated with the other festivals such as *Uisneach* (*Bealtaine*), Loughcrew/*Slíeve na Cailleach* (equinoxes), Tara (mid-summer), Listoghil (*Samhain* sunrise), Mound of the Hostages at Tara (*Samhain* sunrise), Tara (*Lughnasadh* sunset), Dowth (*Samhain/Imbolc* sunset), Newgrange/*Brú Na Bóinne* (winter solstice sunrise), Dowth (winter solstice sunset) plus many more besides. The sunrise and moon rise at *Samhain* forms an alignment from *Tlachtga* to the quartz standing stone in Cairn L of Loughcrew (*Slíeve na Cailleach/Slíeve Bearra*) and Lambay Island (off the coast of Dublin). Interestingly, with the Mound of the Hostages (at Tara) also illuminated by the sunrise at *Samhain*, this alignment continues west across the country, also intersecting 'Lugh's Seat' at the end of the volcanic 'Pillars of *Samhain*' and the cairn of (goddess) *Mór-Ríoghan* above the Keash caves.

So it is clear that in pre-Druidic or proto-Druidic times the people of Ireland constructed sacred sites in stone to mark the astronomically important times of the year, including *Samhain*, the start of the Irish year, during the pagan era. As well as solar festivals the Irish celebrated the lunar events, with Knowth being clearly linked with lunar festivities for the thirteen moons of the year.

Pagan festivities in Ireland were explicitly linked with the agricultural cycle of the year and also with veneration of the gods, the ancestors, the land itself and with the cycle of life and death. These festivals were not just religious events and celebrations, they were social and governmental events – often referred to as an *óenach* (modern Irish *aonach*), or assembly – and still took place still a thousand years after Christianity was introduced to Ireland.

In Ireland the world view was threefold but somewhat different from the modern religious view of Heaven–Earth–Hell. The Irish (and Welsh) pagans believed in three realms – the upperworld (Sky), middleworld (Earth) and otherworld (Sea). The upperworld was the realm of the gods and also spirits that we might liken to angels and demons. The middleworld was the realm of physical existence where we live out our everyday lives. The otherworld was the realm of the dead and also the *sidhe/aos sí* (fairies and *Tuatha Dé Danann*). Strictly speaking, the realm of the dead was not under the sea but beyond the horizon in the west, where the sun sets.

These three realms comprised the known universe and each realm was subdivided again into four or more sections, which are as follows (with thanks to Searles O'Dubhain):

UPPERWORLD – *MAGH MÓR*

Magh Findargat (Plain of White Silver)

Magh Imchiunn (Plain of Gentleness)

Magh Argetnel (Plain of Silver Clouds)

Magh Mel (Plain of Delight)

Magh Airthech (Plain of Bounty)

Magh Ildathach (Plain of Many Colours)

Magh Iongaanaiddh (Plain of Wonders)

Sen Magh (Ancient Plain)

MIDDLEWORLD – *BITH/MIDE*

Aithear – East: associated with the sword of *Nuada*, air, prosperity and change.

Desa – South: associated with the spear of *Lugh*, fire, music and poetry.

Siar – West: associated with the cauldron of *Dagda*, water, knowledge and wisdom.

Thuaidh – North: associated with the stone of destiny (*Lia Fail*), earth, battle and fortitude.

These four objects mentioned are the four treasures of the *Tuatha Dé Danann*, which are also associated with four magical cities – *Findis, Gorias, Murias* and *Falias* (thought not to be in Ireland) – and also with four leaders/Druids – *Uiscias, Eras, Semias* and *Morfesa*.

OTHERWORLD – *TIR ANDOMAIN*

Tir na mBeo (Land of Eternal Life)

Tir na mBan (Land of Women)

Tir fo Thuin (Land Under the Waves)

Tir na n'Og (Land of the Young)

Teach Duinn (House of Donn)

There are various other names, thought to be synonymous with *Tir na n'Og*, such as Isles of the Blessed, Land of Apples, Avalon, etc.

These three realms can be visualised as connected by the *Bile Buadha* or tree of power, otherwise known as the World Tree, which can also be found in other cultures such as Norse, Judaism and in the Americas.

In addition to the three realms, the Irish had a unique view of the human form and also the elements of existence. Evidence would suggest that Druids were well aware of the four elements of neo-Platonic tradition, which fits well with the four directions and four treasures, but they possessed a totally different model based on multiples of three, which unsurprisingly relate to the three realms.

Human	Nature	Direction	Magical Tool	Realm
Head	Heaven	Above	*Torc*	Sky
Brain	Cloud	Through	*Imbas*	Sky
Face	Sun	South	Spear	Sky
Hair	Plants	Outwards	Ogham	Land
Flesh	Earth	Under	Grove	Land
Bone	Stone	North	*Lia Fail*	Land
Mind	Moon	Inwards	Well of *Segais*	Sea
Breath	Wind	East	Sword	Sea
Blood	Sea	West	Cauldron	Sea

So from the above we can see nine elements (*dúile*) in three groups of three that relate both to the human and the wider universe, with each group connected to one of the realms of existence. In addition to this, the nine elements are connected to the three cauldrons within the body. One might think of these as energy centres, similar in concept to the Vedic *chakras*, although the quantity is less (three as opposed to seven).

THREE CAULDRONS

These three cauldrons relate to the health and well-being of a person – once all three are fully upright and boiling away then one could be said to be enlightened. Initially, our cauldrons are sideways and the fire underneath them grows stronger or weaker to reflect the state of each aspect of our health. If your cauldrons are overturned and the fires are out then you are dead!

Cauldron of Knowledge – *Coire Sois*

This resides in the head, the three aspects being head, face and brain, also connected with sky, sun and cloud. This is the centre of wisdom and knowledge, and the ancient Irish also believed that the soul resided in the head.

Cauldron of Vocation – *Coirse Ernmae*

This resides in the centre of the chest, near the heart. The three aspects are flesh, hair and bones, also connected with land, plant and stone. This is the centre of motivation and emotions, love particularly.

Cauldron of Warming – *Coire Goiriath*

This resides in the lower abdomen below the navel. The three aspects are blood, mind and breath, also connected with sea, moon and wind. This is the centre of the physical self, our strength and vitality.

It is possible to work on these three cauldrons spiritually, independently or as a whole, in much the same way that practitioners work on the *chakras.* The three cauldrons are a gateway into the internal life and a key to accessing or revealing *imbas* (insight) through meditation and journeying. They are also an access point into the three realms as experienced shamanically.

Exploring the three realms through journeying is not the remit of this book; that is something that should be studied carefully and extensively, preferably with the help and guidance of an experienced Celtic Shaman or Druid, at least until one has achieved a reasonable level of competency. However, this idea of exploring the three realms does, of course, relate to the otherworld and thereby to *Samhain* – the time of year most strongly associated with the Irish otherworld, the *sidhe* and the ancestors.

Irish stories are full of examples of people visiting the otherworld or those from the otherworld visiting the middleworld – both the fairies, people lost to the fairies and the human dead. In modern Druid practice it is possible to visit all three realms in meditation and journeying (a form of trance), which presumably the ancient Irish were also able to do.

THE CELTIC OTHERWORLD

Somewhat different from the Greek concept of the underworld (Tartarus), it is not a horrible place and it is not visualised as under the earth, although access points, mounds of the *sidhe*, are obviously in the earth. The various places of the Irish otherworld are generally beyond the sea, over the horizon in the west, or sometimes described as beyond the ninth wave (another reference to 3 × 3). It should already be apparent that 3 was the most significant number in the ancient Irish world view – 3 realms, 3 cauldrons, 3 × 3 elements, 3 × 3 body parts, 9 directions. It would make sense for 3 or 9 to factor into where the otherworld is located.

There is some confusion as to whether the otherworld lies in the east (near the Isle of Man) or in the west, in the Atlantic Ocean. The general consensus is that the Irish believed the otherworld (the realm of both the ancestors/dead and the *sidhe)* lay in the west, the place where the sun disappeared to after sunset. This would also make sense given that there is a stretch of water for approximately 3,000 miles west before hitting land again – an infinity of water to the ancient mind. It was believed that when people died their spirit lived on, probably as a physical person, in the otherworld, which was reached via the west through a gateway kept by the ancient Irish god *Donn*.

THE HOUSE OF *DONN*

Donn, meaning 'brown' and also 'dark', was the Irish god of the otherworld. It is often posited that *Donn* is an otherworldly aspect of *Daghdha Mór*, represented as a distant ancestor of all those who die. A particularly insightful mention of *Donn* is in the story 'The Death of *Conaire*' (King *Conaire Mac Mogha Lámha* of Munster). After *Conaire* is slain and his head cut off by two men, three sons of *Donn* (red-headed) come for him. *Donn* is described as 'King of the dead at the red tower of the dead' and the three sons ride three horses of *Donn* – saying, 'although we are alive, we are dead!' A ninth-century text referring to *Donn* states, 'To me, to my house, you shall come after your death.'

Skellig Michael, off the Iveragh Peninsula in west Kerry, has become associated with *Donn* via a story of the Milesians burying the commander (*Donn*) of a ship of twenty-four on the island, although elsewhere he is named *Ir*. This may be an ancient confusion with Bull Rock, also in Kerry, or perhaps both places served a similar purpose.

In ancient times Bull Rock (*Teach Duinn*) off the west Kerry coast was the house of *Donn*, from where the dead would be taken into the otherworld. It was the place 'where the dead assemble'. In addition to Bull Rock, two other locations are given as the residing place of *Donn*, in folk tradition: *Cnoc Fírinne* (in Co. Limerick) and, more similar to Bull Rock, Dunbeg on the west coast of Co. Clare. Stories of *Donn* persisted into the Christian era, with legends of him abducting people, riding out on horseback like the Norse Odin and even being confused with the ghost of the Earl of Desmond (*Gearóid Iarla Mhic Gearailt*).

MANANNÁN MAC LÍR

Donn was not the only god associated with the otherworld and death. *Manannán* is associated with the sea but also with the otherworld. It is he that is associated with carrying the dead into the afterlife and also the mythical isle where he lived. The Isle of Man (*Mana*) between Britain and Ireland is named after him. Anglesey (*Mona*) is associated with *Manannán*, as is *Aran*, off the coast of Scotland. All of these islands are to the east of Ireland, causing the confusion over whether the otherworld lies in the east or the west. His island home was not necessarily in the otherworld itself, although he was said to rule over *Magh Meall* (The Pleasant Plain), which is clearly part of the otherworld, as are *Tir Tairngire* (Land of Promise) and *Eamhan Abhalach* (Region of Apples), which he is also associated with.

As with *Donn*, *Manannán* is associated with horses, particularly *Enbharr* (meaning water foam), a horse that could pull a chariot over the waves. *Manannán* had many properties, a crane bag of useful magical items, magical otherworldly apples and he produced demi-god offspring in Ireland and is associated with *Brú Na Bóinne*/*Síd in Broga*/Newgrange.

Manannán is also described in a Manx ballad as the first owner of the Isle of Man, called *Ellan Sheeant* (meaning otherworld island) which he could conceal from passing vessels with a magic mist.

Skellig Michael (*Sceilig Mhichíl*), off the west Kerry coast, is also associated with him. The first historical reference to the Skelligs occurs in legend when it is given as the burial place of *Ir*, son of *Míl*, who was drowned during the landing of the Milesians in Ireland. The settlement perched on top of Skellig Michael is generally regarded as having been built by Christian monks, but there is no real proof of this. It is equally possible that this remote island stuck out in the Atlantic was used by their pagan predecessors. It is quite likely that the connection of *Manannán* to this place is in regard to the otherworld and it was a gathering place of the dead, like Bull Rock. Indeed, Skellig Michael may well have also been associated with *Donn* at one time, but this is impossible to prove. Personally, I think that Skellig Michael was used before the Christian era as a staging post for the souls of the dead and was probably used by the Druids and perhaps noble or royal persons in relation to death. Because of the lack of archaeological evidence, this theory is impossible to prove or disprove – however, it would fit with the general theme of a psycho-pomp island in the western ocean and with the common practice of Christian hierarchy taking over existing pagan sites and repurposing them for their own intentions.

CAILLEACH

The hag or veiled one is most well known in Kerry, particularly the Beare Peninsula, which is split between Kerry and Cork (mostly Cork). She is the main goddess in Ireland associated with death, the otherworld and winter. She also has an ancient site – Loughcrew or *Slíeve na Calliagh* (Co. Meath) is named after her, which is probably one of the oldest sacred monuments in Ireland, with evidence of now disappeared building works from long before the current, very ancient complex was built.

Interestingly, the *Cailleach* is associated with the west, it being said she was born in the most westerly house in Ireland (*Teach Mór*) on the Dingle Peninsula (*Corca Dhuibhne*), which ties in with links to the otherworld and the dead departing into the west. She is linked with the sovereignty of the land, the coming of winter, the ancestors of the 'tribe' and the otherworld, perhaps having had a similar role to *Donn* and *Manannán*. She is also found in Scotland, probably introduced by Irish colonists in the late pagan era.

SAMHAIN

The festival of *Samhain* is generally regarded as the most important of the eight by modern pagans and is also regarded as the pagan New Year. It would appear to have been the start of the year in pre-Christian times too, but whether or not it was regarded as the most important festival is impossible to say.

From what has been covered in this chapter, it is clear that the otherworld was an important part of the Irish pagan worldview and that several important deities were associated with death and the souls of the dead – primarily in the western ocean or islands on the edge of it.

Even if *Samhain* did not have quite the glamour and interest as Halloween does today, it would be unlikely to be as trivialised and superficial as this modern festival has largely become. Ancient peoples took death very seriously, the Gaulish, British and Irish pagans being no exception to that. Death today is perhaps more shocking in that it is a less frequent occurrence due to the staving off of disease, famine and constant warfare. Nonetheless, the ancient Celtic peoples were well aware of their fragility and the ever-present threat of death either through battle or by natural causes.

Samhain was the entry point into winter, a time of hardship, cold and hunger, especially for those who had not made the necessary preparations. It was also a time of introspection, of communing with the dead and the otherworld – themes that have somehow survived, albeit distorted, into the modern era.

Depiction of one of the sidhe (fairies) at a ring fort.

CHAPTER 2

The Festival of Samhain

'All Saints' Day perpetuated the Pagan Samhain of November Eve'
James Bonwick, 1894

While most modern people have little notion of *Samhain*, if they have even heard of it, it has played an important role in Irish life for millennia, and in the form of Halloween it still does today. We can go back into the ancient past through old Irish texts and the wonders of archaeology but there is actually still a wealth of extant folk practices that are either still in existence now or have been recorded in relatively recent times (in Celtic countries), such as this quote from 1889:

November Eve is sacred to The Spirits of the Dead. In the western islands the old superstition is dying very hard, and tradition is still well alive. It is dangerous to be out on November Eve, because it is the one night in the year when the dead come out of their graves to dance with the fairies on the hills, and it is their night, they do not like to be disturbed … Funeral games are held in their houses.

Mrs S. Bryant, *Celtic Ireland*

Samhain is the modern Irish (*Gaeilge*) name for the month of November, thought to be derived from *sam-fuin*, meaning the end of summer. It is probably no accident that 1 November is All Souls' Day in the Christian calendar – placed there to override and wipe out its pagan predecessor. *Samhain* became known, in English, as November Eve or as Halloween, which is short for the Eve of All Hallows' Day. A ninth-century text states (*as Gaeilge/in* Irish), 'the saints of the teeming world enoble stormy Samhain'.

The modern Irish name for Halloween is not *Samhain* but *Oíche Shamhna*, which means the 'Eve of November' or 'November Night'.

The exact date of the original *Samhain* is subject to some controversy as a result of the change from the *Gaeilge* calendar to the Roman Catholic Church's Gregorian calendar, which moves the traditional days by up to ten days, which is why New Year is not at the winter solstice. Some say that Old Halloween or true *Samhain* falls around 5/6/7 November. According to the website Archaeoastronomy.com, true *Samhain* fell on 7 November in 2020. Whether this is true or not, *Samhain* marks the pivotal point in the Gaelic year, the threshold between the summer and winter halves of the year (*Tráth na Táirsí*). With winter preceding summer, the old year ends and the new year begins at *Samhain*.

Almost all modern pagans celebrate *Samhain* on 31 October, the date of Halloween, with only a tiny minority opting for the later date. Opinions vary, but some believe that the ancient *Samhain* was celebrated over three days, while some suggest that the whole month of November was regarded as a liminal time of significance.

References to *Samhain* can be found going back into the stories of the pagan era. For instance, from 'The Wooing of Étain' (translated by John Carey):

'What advice do you give this boy [*Oengus*]?' said *Midir*. 'I have some for him,' said *Eochaid*. 'At *Samhain* let him go into the *Bruig*, and let him bring weapons with him. That is a day of peace and concord among the men of Ireland; none fears his neighbour then.'

From 'The Boyhood Deeds of *Finn*' (translated by Kuno Meyer):

The men of Ireland were contending for the girl (Éile); each in turn would go to woo her. The wooing used to be undertaken every year at *Samhain*, for the *síde* of Ireland were always open at *Samhain*, for at *Samhain* no concealment could be upon the *síde* …

While *Finn* was there on the night of *Samhain* he saw the two *síde* – that is the two strongholds – laid bare around him after their concealing enchantment (*fé fíada*) had dissolved. He saw a great fire in each of the two strongholds, and heard a voice from one of them saying, 'Is your sweet food (*suabais*) good?'

These quotations, and many since lost documents, were written down during the Christian period, however, it is hard to tell at what point they were first committed to ink – what we have today are undoubtedly copies of copies that were originally written purely in Old Irish. Much of what we have to work from today is in medieval Irish or a mixture of the two, from which to translate into either modern Irish or English. Statements that the pagans had no literature and could not write are disproven by the works of the Christians themselves. It has been stated that the Druids in Ireland could speak and write ancient Greek; it is also recorded that St Patrick destroyed more than 400 pagan books by burning them – if the pagans had been illiterate, this would not have been necessary! Also, in the *Annals of the Four Masters*, it is stated that *Cormac Mac Art* ordered that all the knowledge of the land be written down into books. He is believed to have lived around 200 CE, so one can assume that writing existed in Ireland quite some time before that.

One can be fairly certain that the Irish could read and write long before the establishment of Christian monasteries, and that the Irish were not the illiterate people in the manner that Christian hagiography has described them. This being the case, we can be fairly confident that some or all of the accounts of pre-Christian belief and practices are at least partially based in truth and some may in fact have been passed down from both oral and written records from the pagan era.

Samhain marked the time of the return to darkness, the forces of life being absorbed into the earth or into the otherworld and a state of death or hibernation occurring until spring returned at *Imbolc*. It was at *Samhain* that final harvests were collected and any excess livestock were ritually slaughtered for feasting, as offerings and also food was preserved for the winter. To this day, it is supposed that picking blackberries after Halloween is bad luck – folklore has it that the Devil or *Púca* (a not-so-nice fairy) has spat on them, or worse still, urinated on them.

As indicted in the ancient texts, it was thought that the boundary between the everyday realm of earth and the otherworld became thin, or even non-existent, at this time, with the *sidhe* and the dead being able to easily penetrate into the human world. In later Christian times, it was believed that the dead, the fairies and *Tuatha Dé Danann* would run amok and cause mischief if they weren't placated and paid the proper respect.

OFFERINGS/SACRIFICES

Offerings were made in the form of oat cakes and libations of milk. Barmbrac (also barm brac, barmbrack or *bairín breac*) or Halloween brac is a cake still eaten today that may have had some connection with this tradition but it is also linked with divination and good luck. Sacrificial offerings were made to help ensure the return of the forces of life in the spring and to ward off negative actions by the *sidhe*, the gods and to deter blight and famine. Sacrificing a pig was common in ancient times and it is postulated that earlier still humans were sacrificed. Bog burials in Ireland exhibit ritually slain people who do not appear to be of the lowest classes. Perhaps the idea of the corrupt or incompetent ruler leading to the suffering of the people and the land was reversed by their own death?

In order to protect the home and people, various herbs were used – rosemary, vervain, rowan, mugwort and others. Iron pins were often worn by people in order to keep the *sidhe* away. Another form of protection involves the sacrifice of a live chicken. This has survived into modern times in the act called 'bleeding for St Martin'. On St Martin's Day (11 November) people ritually slit the throat of a chicken in honour of St Martin and spray a wall of the house, all the walls or the corners of the house with the chicken's blood, although often a cockerel is used rather than a hen. This practice has been observed being done by elderly people in current times. This subject has been explored extensively by Professor Billy Mag Fhionn in his book *Blood Rites: The Feast of St Martin in Ireland*:

Maguelonne Toussaint-Samat, in *A History of Food*, claims the killing of geese at St Martin's Day was a relic of more ancient practices to do with Samhain, and that it represented the practice, as she puts it, of 'eating the god'. Véronique Guibert de la Vayssiere also drew close parallels with St Martin's Day and the ancient festival of *Samhain*, portraying St Martin as inheriting mythological associations from ancient Celtic beliefs.

The fourteenth-century account of pigs being offered as tribute at Martinmas gives evidence of a change in Irish custom, particularly under the influence of the Anglo-Normans. Rent and tribute that was paid at *Samhain* under the Gaelic system can be seen to be paid instead at St Martin's Day under the new economic model of the Anglo-Normans. The transference of fairs and assemblies from *Samhain* to Martinmas was also part of this process of change, where the important commercial day at the end of summer was moved from November 1st to November 11th. Thus, the practical economic customs of slaughter of animals and the feasting on their meat changed context. The popular sayings regarding 'nine nights and a night' express a widespread association of *Samhain* with St Martin's Day, particularly in more Gaelic areas. In addition, it was widely believed that the period between the two feasts was the appropriate time in which to spill blood, but never after November 11th.

Joe McGowan, in his book *Echoes of a Savage Land*, describes in gruesome detail how this rite was performed, writing at the turn of the twenty-first century:

Blood was spattered everywhere. Bright red droplets smeared the whitewashed wall, dripping from the feathered head and forming puddles in the muddy street … Like the sombre shadow of the grim reaper, an old woman watched the death struggles of the cockerel … The burnished steel of the bloodstained knife in her hand reflected the glow of a blood-red harvest sun dropping serenely into the turbulent Atlantic beyond Inismurray Island.

One of the churches dedicated to him [St Martin] is the ruined *Teampall Liath* within the enclosure of an earthen *lios*, located near the railway line at Lispole station in County Kerry. A 'pattern' (patron day or day of pilgrimage) was held there at one time, and another at St Martin's Well on the road to Dingle. Visits to these sites were believed to be very effective in the curing of diseases concerning cattle, with the old proviso that any animal so cured must be slaughtered on the following St Martin's Eve.

The above describes a tradition that appears to have migrated from *Samhain* to St Martin's Eve, with the theme of ritual slaughter enduring into the modern era.

DIVINATION

Since ancient times *Samhain* has been associated with prophesy and divination. The Druids were well known to perform divination. One particular form, *Tarbhfeis*, involved eating the flesh of a dog and the Druid being wrapped in a bull's hide to aid their clairvoyance while in a sleep/ trance. Irish mythology is full of portents and predictions and the Druids are recorded in the Irish texts as having at least three types of divination they undertook – *Imbas Forosnai*, *Teinm Laida* and *Dichetal do Chennaib* – all of which are described in *Cormac's Glossary*. *Samhain* was considered the most opportune time for divination and it was also a time when the whole country gathered in celebration, with the most important people being gathered together at Tara for the feast and assembly of *Samhain*.

The Barmbrac, still eaten today, contains a metal ring, and the person who finds it when eating is said (depending on tradition) to be destined to be married by next *Samhain* or receive especially good luck. The Scottish bannock is a variant on the same theme: in Scotland and northern England, a girl would bake a bannock cake in the evening. In complete silence, she walked to her room and would place the bannock under her pillow. Her dreams that night would show her the face of her future lover or husband, and in the morning she would eat the bannock. Various games associated with *Samhain* are in fact derived from ancient divination practices.

SACRED FIRES

The bonfire is a recurring theme within Celtic festivals, particularly in Ireland. Ceremonies centred on the lighting of the winter fires are said to originate from *Lugh Lámfhota* (the *Tuatha Dé Danann* hero of the second battle of Moytura and later on also High King) around 1450 BCE. This being the case, the tradition of sacred fires in Ireland is some 3,500 years old. Fire seems to be have been used at all eight of the pagan festivals, most notably at *Bealtaine* (two fires), the summer solstice and at *Samhain*.

The Halloween bonfire can be traced all the way back to the ancient festival at Tara, held every *Samhain*. All fires were extinguished all over Ireland before the sunset. The sacred fire was supposedly lit by the Druids at *Tlachtga* and brought to Tara where the king, nobility and Druids presided over the lighting of the fire. After the Tara fire was lit, fires were lit all over the country symbolising the offering of warmth and protection through the dark months of the year, at its entry point.

A similar act happened at *Bealtaine* with the twin fires being lit at Tara by the king and his entourage. This act was of great symbolic value, which is exactly why St Patrick lit a fire at *Bealtaine* on the Hill of Slane, in advance of the Tara fire being lit (given as around Easter by Church accounts). It was an outrage, and a direct challenge to the existing order that has been in Ireland for perhaps thousands of years. As we know, Patrick was subsequently successful in winning over King Laoghaire, the Irish High King.

However, in contradiction to the common view, Ireland did not become Christian almost overnight. In truth, it took about 300 years for the whole country to convert to Christianity, which is evidenced by both legends and archaeological evidence from graves. As a result, the transition to Christianity involved the retention of many of the cultural norms of the pagan religion and administration. The sacred fire stayed; although it was no longer part of pagan ceremony, it remained of vital importance in the celebration of the now Christianised seasonal festivals.

The sacred fire continued to be used at *Samhain* and is still common in modern-day celebrations, whether secular or religious. This tradition extends beyond Ireland, into Britain but the date of the bonfire celebrations was moved to 5 November after the Catholic gunpowder plot of 1605. As a result of the attempt to kill James I and his parliament, 'bonfire night' is celebrated on the anniversary of the failed assassination in Britain. It has also been common to burn effigies of Guido Fawkes and also the Pope on the fires, something that still happens today, particularly in Protestant parts of Northern Ireland.

To a large extent, the original sacred meaning of the fires at all eight of the festivals has been lost. Certainly in Britain this is true, and in Ireland the main use of a bonfire remains at May Day (*Lá Bealtaine*) and Halloween (*Oíche Shamhna*). Although somewhat detached from the original meaning, the custom still persists.

Games & Tricks

It was common for young people, until recent times, to go out and cause havoc and harmless mischief in impersonation of the spirits of the dead and the *sidhe*, who could be capricious. This has clearly evolved into the modern tradition of 'trick or treat'. It is well known that games took place at the *aonach,* or assembly, and *Samhain* was no exception, so the idea of games that has survived into the modern era is undoubtedly derived from the ancient games held at *Samhain*, although we have no real accounts of what those games were. Coupled with the interest in divination at this time, some of the games that developed or survived into the modern era are 'divination games' such as ducking for apples. Much of the games persisted into the Christian era but by the mid-twentieth century many of them were no longer taking place. Fortunately, there are records of what they involved, which are explored in Chapter 5.

Coming of the Dead

As a time devoted to the dead (the ancestors), it was common to set a place at the dinner table for the departed. In some cases food was left on the plate as an actual, rather than symbolic, offering that would be left overnight. Candles were lit in the window(s) to help guide the spirits of the ancestors to the family home. Windows and doors were also left ajar to aid the spirits of the family dead to enter the home. As it was considered that the *ráths* and ancient burial mounds were portals or entry/exit points between the middleworld and the otherworld, offerings were often left at mounds and *ráths*.

Failure to make appropriate gestures to the ancestors at *Samhain* was considered to be bad luck and disrespect could lead to a person being ostracised. For instance, a person who ate the food left for ancestors would be barred from participating in the *Samhain* festivities. It was also considered that after their own death, they would not be able to return to their descendants to participate at *Samhain* – a quite considerable punishment. It was also thought that those who did not throw out dirty water and damp down the fire could be attacked by unwanted spirits of the dead.

There is a vast treasure trove of lore relating to the *sidhe* riding out, the wild hunt, the fairies running amok and the king of the fairies gallivanting across the land at *Samhain*. These stories change down the ages and many variants of similar legends and ghost stories exist. An early example of such a story is that of *Eachtra Nera*, in which *Nera* (a Connacht warrior) enters the otherworld via a *ráth* of the *Tuatha Dé Danann*. In some legends the dead or the fairies ride out on horses causing havoc, and to be out alone on *Samhain* night is to risk being killed or abducted by them!

Belief that the dead could rise is clearly evidenced by the story 'The Recovery of the Tain' (*Do fallsigud Tána bó Cualnge*), from the *Book of Leinster*, in which the ghost of Fergus is raised. The story takes place during the reign of Guaire, the King of Connacht, at which time the epic story (*Táin Bó Cúailnge*) was known in fragments and was incomplete:

There, however, the poets of Ireland were summoned by *Senchán Torpeist* to see if they had the *Tain Bo Cualnge* in its entirety in their memory. And they said they knew only parts of it. *Senchán* then asked who among his students would go with his blessing to the land of Letha to learn the *Táin* which the sage had taken away to the east instead of the *Culmen*. This suited *Emine hua Ninene* and *Muirgein* son of *Senchán* to go to the east.

They travelled to the grave of *Fergus mac Roig* and to his stone at Énloch in Connacht. *Murgein* sat alone against the stone of *Fergus*, and the others left to seek, in the meantime, a home for them. However *Murgein* sang a poem to the stone, as if it were to *Fergus* himself that he was addressing, in which [?] then he said this: 'If this is not a stone ••• o *Fergus!*'

Then a great mist rose around him, so that its people did not find him until the end of three days and three nights. So *Fergus* went to him, in very nice clothe, viz, a green garment, a coat with a hood decorated with red [threads], a gold-hilted sword, bronze shoes, his brown hair round him. *Fergus* told him all the *Táin* as it took place from the beginning to the end. But others say it was proclaimed to *Senchán* after he fasted against the race of *Fergus*, and it would not be surprising that this is true. Then all returned to *Senchán* and told him their trip, and he was then very pleased with them for that.

Here is the enumeration of the tales which precede the *Tain Bo Cualnge*, namely, all twelve: the Taking of the *Sid*, the Dream of *Oengus*, the Quarrel of the two Pig Keepers, the Cattle-Raid of *Regamna*, the Adventures of *Nera*, the Birth of *Conchobar*, the Courtship of *Ferb*, the Birth of *Cuchulainn*, the Driving of the Cattle of *Flidais*, The Courtship of *Emer*. They also say that there would be in the preliminary tales: the march of *Cuchulainn* to the house of *Culann* the smith; how *Cuchulainn* took his weapons and how he went with the chariot; how *Cuchulainn* went to join the boys in *Emain Macha*. But these last three stories are told in the course of the *Táin*.

From the *Book of Leinster*, translated by Erik Stohellou.

SAMHAIN AT TARA

It is well recorded that *Samhain* was celebrated in ancient times at the hill of Tara. Perhaps the oldest story we have of *Samhain* is *Echtra Nera* (The Adventures of Nera), which was preserved in two versions, one translated by Egerton in 1782 and the other used by Kuno Meyer, along with the first, to give a complete translation in 1889:

> One Halloween *Ailill* and *Medb* were in *Rath Cruachan* with their whole household. They set about cooking food. Two captives had been hanged by them the day before that. Then *Ailill* said: 'He who would now put a withe round the foot of either of the two captives that are on the gallows, shall have a prize for it from me, as he may choose.'
>
> Great was the darkness of that night and its horror, and demons would appear on that night always. Each man of them went out in turn to try that night, and quickly would he come back into the house. 'I will have the prize from thee,' said *Nera*, 'and I shall go out.' 'Truly thou shalt have this my gold-hilted sword here', said *Ailill*.

Ailill, King of Connacht, offers a prize to whoever would tie a *withe* (rag/twig) around one of the dead men's leg. *Nera* is brave enough to take on this task and has a conversation with one of the dead men, who asks for a drink. Due to the practice of *Smáladh na Tine* (covering the fire), the house is protected from the spirits of the otherworld (by a ring of invisible fire) and another house is protected by a ring of water as they have thrown out the dirty water earlier. A third house is unprotected and *Nera* and the hanged man are able to enter for water. The hanged man throws dirty water on the faces of the sleeping occupants, causing them to die.

When *Nera* returns to *Ráth Cruachan* it has been set alight by the *Tuatha Dé Danann* who have ridden out their *sí/sidhe* in the cave of *Cruachan* to do so. *Nera* secretly returns to their *sidhe* with them, meets the king of the *sidhe*, gains a wife and, after a short return to the human world, returns forever to live in the *sidhe*.

While this story takes place a long distance from Tara, it demonstrates the importance of the *Samhain* safety precautions, the belief in the return of the dead, the riding out of the *sidhe* and the ability to enter and leave the otherworld.

More direct references to *Samhain* at Tara are given below, from 'The Birth of *Áed Sláine*' translated by *Máirin Ní Dhonnchadha*:

> It was common practice moreover for the men of Ireland to come from every quarter to Tara to partake of the Feast of Tara at *Samain*. For the two renowned gatherings which the men of Ireland had, were the Feast of Tara every *Samain* for that was the pagans' Easter, and the Fair at *Tailtiu* every *Lughnasad*. During the course of the year, no-one dared infringe any penalty or law that was ordained by the men of Ireland at either of those dates.

And from 'The Death of *Diarmait Mac Cerbaill*' (translated by John Carey):

> After that *Diarmait* went on his royal circuit sunwise around Ireland. For this is how the king of Tara used to go through Ireland: from Tara into Leinster, from there into Munster, from there into Connacht, and finally into Ulster; so that he would return to Tara at the end of the year's time, at *Samain*, to spend

Aerial view of the Hill of Tara, seat of the Irish High Kings.

Samain with the men of Ireland, celebrating the *Feis Temro* (Feast of Tara), associated with the confirmation of the king.

A later tale, from the *Fiannaíocht* (*Fionn*) Cycle, *Agallamh na Seanórach* (translated by Whitely Stokes and E. Windisch, 1900), describes how *Fionn Ma Cumhail* defeats the *Tuatha Dé Danann* leader *Ailléan* from a fairy mound at *Sliabh gCullinn* in Armagh. The action begins at the feast of *Samhain* in Tara at the palace of *Conn Céadchathach*, *Ard Rí* (High King). Every year *Ailléan* rides down, with his host, to ruin the *Samhain* celebrations by burning down all the (wooden) buildings. With the aid of a magical poisonous spear from *Faicha Mac Congha*, *Fionn* is able to hunt down and kill *Ailléan*, piercing him through the heart, and then returning to claim his prize from the *Ard Rí*, which is to become the leader of the *Fianna Éireann* (Warband of Ireland).

According to *General History of Ireland* (*Foras Feasa ar Éirinn*) by Geoffrey Keating (completed in 1634), Tara (*Temair*) was built by *Ard Rí Tuathai Techmar* (after whom it is supposedly named) after the creation of the central kingdom of *Mide* at the beginning of the first millennium CE. He was said to have constructed *Tlachtga*, *Tailtin* (Teltown) and *Uisneach* as well around the same time, with each fortress constructed from part of an existing kingdom. Keating's history has proven to be somewhat unreliable and archaeological evidence would suggest that Tara was an important centre as long ago as 2500 BCE, which makes a mockery of his assertion regarding the origin of Tara. The same can be said of all three other sites – the story Keating referred to was clearly an attempt by *Tuathai Techmar* or his followers to appropriate these important sites for his own fame and notoriety.

St Patrick is recorded to have visited Tara in 433 CE before temporarily returning to Rome. There is no record of him having visited *Tlachtga*, the centre of paganism in Ireland, although he is said to have baptised the

Luigni tribe who lived exactly in the area where *Tlachtga* is located. If he did not visit *Tlachtga* itself he must have passed within a few miles. Folk tradition in the area is that Patrick did in fact visit *Tlachtga* and it is said that the early Christian church about half a mile away was established by him (*Timpeal Cuimhneas*). While this may be true, there is no written (or even oral) story of his visit to what was undoubtedly one the most important places in Ireland at that time.

With the onset of Christianity, the festival of All Saints was introduced to Ireland in the seventh century. The date was changed to 1 November by a Church decree in 835 CE in order to supplant the still functional pagan day of the dead, *Samhain*. This change seemed to have little effect on the celebrations at Tara and across the country, which led to the introduction of All Souls Day in 988 CE.

In 1168 the last recorded celebrations of *Samhain* took place at Tara under the last *Ard Rí* of Ireland – *Ruadri Ua Conchobair*. Following the Norman invasion, in May 1169 the meetings of the Irish royalty were disrupted and never resumed; in 1183 *Ruadri Ua Conchobair* abdicated as High King of Ireland.

Up until this point (1169), Tara was the most important cultural centre of Ireland – it was where the High King sat and where the four or five provincial kings met each other and the High King. It was where the major feasts were celebrated and in particular, *Samhain* was always celebrated at Tara. Tara symbolised the High Kings, the unity of the four (at one time five) provinces and still even now symbolises the sovereignty of Ireland, but it was not the religious centre of Ireland. The religious centre of Ireland, at least for 1,000 years before the birth of Jesus of Nazareth, was in fact *Tlachtga*, a few miles away. *Tlachtga* was the home of the Druids of Ireland and seemingly their most sacred place. It was from here that the Druids brought the sacred flame on every *Oíche Shamhna*, after the sun had set, to light the royal fire at Tara.

The Mound of the Hostages, at the Hill of Tara, has a Samhain alignment.

CHAPTER 3

Tlachtga and Mogh Ruith

TLACHTGA

Tlachtga is the ancient name for what is now the Hill of Ward, close to the small town of Athboy, in Co. Meath, a county that is full of important, impressive monuments and ruins from the early Christian era and the pagan era, reaching back thousands of years. So, that begs the question where does the name *Tlachtga* come from?

Tlachtga was undoubtedly a woman – depending on the sources you refer to, she is either a Druidess, daughter of the Druid *Mogh Ruith* or she is an ancient goddess. According to John Gilroy in *Tlachtga: Celtic Fire Festival*, the name is comprised of two compounds. The first part, *tlacht*, means 'earth' in English and may be related to the modern Irish words for 'earth', *talamh* and *talún*. From this it has been suggested that she was some form of earth goddess.

The second part of the name, *ga*, has various interpretations such as 'ray', 'spear', 'sting' or 'dart'. This may in a certain context be similar to the magical weapon of the demi-god hero *Cuchulainn*, the *Gae Bulga*, which was not really a spear – it had a unique shape, but was thrown like a spear and was an invincible weapon. From these two components we get the name 'earth-spear' or 'earth-ray', in either case it could be connected with lightning, which the ancient Irish supposed was related to solar power, coming from the gods. Lightning can be likened to both a spear or a ray of light hitting the earth, so perhaps *Tlachtga* may have been a goddess of lightning or of the sun? Having no written evidence to fully explain her name, one can only speculate.

There are several stories relating to this goddess, the most recent being that of the medieval *Metrical Dindsenchas* (place lore in verse form) and *banshenchas* (women's lore), both of which refer to *Tlachtga* and also her father *Mogh Ruith/Mog Roith*. In both of these Christianised stories *Mogh Ruith* is cast as being a student of Simon Magus, and also the stories describe Magus' three sons either having consensual sex with or raping her at *Imbolc*. It is said that *Tlachtga* gave birth to triplets at *Samhain*, dying in childbirth and leaving her name to the site where she gave birth and died. Here are two versions of the story:

Tlachtga and *Mogh Ruith* (Kilbride MS 3, Advocates' Library, Edinburgh):

> *Tlachtgha* whence named? *Moghruith* [the wizard's] daughter *Tlachtgha*, whom (when with her father she went to study magic in the eastern world) Simon Magus's sons all three had to wife, even she it was that for *Trén* constructed the *roth rámhach*, the flagstone that is *Forchartha*, and the cauldron in *Cnámchoill*. Then she, bringing with her these two last, returned out of the East and reached [the present] *tulach Tlachtgha*; here she lay in and three sons were born: *Dorib*, a quo *mágh nDoirbi*; *Cuma*, a quo *mágh gCuma*; *Muach*, a quo *mágh Muaich*; so long as which names subsist in the men of Erin's memory, vengeance of outside strangers shall not attain Ireland. She died in childbed and over her the *dún* was erected, hence *Tlachtgha*.

Tlachtga (*Metrichal Dindshenchas*, translated by Edward Gwynn) provides both a poem and 'prose':

Tlachtga, dignified, noble hillock,
[place of] completion of kings with great valour,
that long ago belonged to fair *Tlachtga*,
daughter of the pure *Moga* [slave] of king *Roith*.

Mug Roith son of *Fergusa Fáil*
son of royal, devout *Rossa*,
Cacht daughter of *Chathmind* of the feats
[was] his mother lovely-complexioned, reliable.

Roth son of *Riguill* fostered him;
so he was taken as *Mug Roith* [*Roth*'s slave]:
Moga's two sons were *Búan* and *Corb*,
lucky for the host was their noble-chanting.

The mother of these sons was
Derdraigen, severe, ruthless,
and mother of fair *Cairpri*,
who is surely gentle as bardcraft's flower.

Moga's daughter, assembly of thousands,
chosen *Tlachtga*, not cold her form,
went with her great and beloved father
to noble *Símón* sechtmisid [lit. 'seven months' child'].

Three sons had *Símón*, they were at ease,
vast their devilish undertaking,

Nero, Carpent and Uetir,
they were a powerful people, always in strife.

Together the sons gave
love to *Tlachtga* through secrecy,
cast their seed into her womb, without exaggeration,
with fitting children of equal size.

Tlachtga one of the three, not feeble,
she made the red wheel, greatly-strong,
together with great and beloved *Mug*
and with Símón sechtmisid.

She takes the remainder, I know,
Left behind by the wheel's track,
a perfect stone in weak *Forcarthain*,
and the standing stone in *Cnámchaill.*

Totally blind each one who beholds with his eye,
deaf each one who hears it,
dead any because of the thing,
the wheel rough-bristling points.

After arriving from the east
carrying three sons of great-beauty:
the bright spirited lady dies at the time of birthing:
a great story without concealing the hearing.

The names of her sons, told without restriction,
Múach and *Chuma* and fair *Doirb*:

the assembly of *Thoraig*, possessed them,
to them (and their safety) was proclaimed.

Long enduring fame over *Banba's* renown
as long as the names of her sons endure,
the true story from there is spread,
no quenching will come to her people.

The grave-mound was dug on the hill
of the woman of the very-cold region
among every high-name of a lucky sage
is the high-name of silent *Tlachtga*.

Tlachtga, proud and princely hill, has seen the passing of many a
stern king, since long ago seemly *Tlachtga* possessed it, daughter
of the famous slave of kingly *Roth*.

Mug Roith was son of *Fergus Fail*, son of royal and worshipful
Ross; *Cacht* daughter of *Cathmann* skilled in feats was his own
mother, fresh of hue.

Roth son of *Rigoll* fostered him, therefore was he *Roth's* chosen
slave: his two sons were *Buan* and *Corb*, whose noble chant
brought the people luck.

The mother of those goodly sons was *Derdraigen*, strong, fierce, and
fell: she was mother too of *Cairpre*, as my gentle bardic art certifies.

Daughter of *Mug*, master of thousands, was choice *Tlachtga* –
not chill was her bosom: with her giant father dear went she to
noble Simon sechtmisid.

Three sons had Simon, who dwelt at ease; gigantic was their
league of hell: Nero, Carpent, and Uetir, they were a mighty race,
mortal in conflict.

All the sons together gave their love to *Tlachtga* secretly, and quickened her womb, in truth, with offspring like in build and bulk.

Tlachtga – no weakling was she – was one of three, with the beloved giant slave and with Simon sechtmisid, who made the red well-finished Wheel.

She carried with her the fragment, *I wis*, that the cunningly lade Wheel left behind it, the perfect Stone at feeble *Forcarthain* and the Pillar at *Cnamchaill*.

Blind is each that once sees it, deaf is each that hears it: dead he that aught touches of the rough-jagged dreadful Wheel.

When the woman came westward she bore three sons of great beauty: she died at their birth, the bright brisk lady : a strange lie – let us hear it and hide it not!

The names of her sons (no meagre utterance) were *Muach* and *Cumma* and darling *Doirb*: 'tis for the men of *Torach*, that claimed them for its own, to hear their names – and mark ye them!

In these texts we see *Tlachtga's* story tied to that of *Mogh Ruith* who, like her, is a rather mysterious character who also needs some exploration in order to see clearly what is going on in the mythology. The language used here is somewhat ambiguous and it is not entirely clear if *Tlachtga* was raped by the sons of Simon Magus, but this does appear the most likely interpretation. However, in the following text, it is quite clear that *Tlachtga* was raped by the sons:

Tlachtga, Book of Ballymote (RIA MS 23 p.12, col. 406):

Why was *Tlachtga* so called? Not difficult. *Tlachtga* was the daughter of *Mog Roith*, son of Fergus. Three sons of the magician

Simon raped her. She went with her father to learn the magic arts practised anywhere in the world. And it was she who made for Trian the Rolling Wheel, the stone in *Forcathu* and the Pillar in *Cnamchaill*. She came from the East and brought with her these things until she reached the hills of *Tlachtga*. It was there she bore three sons, *Doirb*, *Cumma* and *Muach*, who gave their names to three regions. As long as their names are remembered in Ireland the land will not be visited by vengeful strangers. It is said of *Tlachtga*:

Tlachtga Hills, splendid and high,
Foreboding doom to a great, unswerving king
Before the step which Tlachtga … took,
The daughter of King Roth's clever votary.
Mog Roith, the son of Fergus Fal,
The kingly and noble son of Ross.
Cacht, the daughter of the quarrelsome Catmend
Was his colourful arid noble mother.
Roth, son of Rigoll was his fosterer.
This is why the name 'Mog Roith' was given him.
Two sons of Mog: Buan and Fer-Corb,
Were successful over armies in deeds of liberation.
She [Cacht] was the [foster] mother of the handsome sons
Of Der-Droighen, dark, strong and active,
And the real mother of Cairpre [Lifechair].
It is certain that he deceived the Hui-Bairdne.
The daughter of Mog hosted with thousands,
Tlachtga, the chosen – not that she was without feelings
To accompany her great and noble father,
To noble Simon of sevenfold splendour.

Three sons had Simon pleasing to look upon:
Sorrowful her struggle with their devilry.
… [text missing] … powerful.
Theirs was a powerful family, vehement and resilient.
The sons grew passionate Towards Tlachtga at the same time,
They flowed into her body – it is no lie
making] descendants of beauty and lineage.
For Trian it was no honour
Tlachtga Created the red and swiftly mobile wheel,
Together with the great and noble Mog,
And with Simon of sevenfold splendour.
She brought with her wise sayings;
She left the moving wheel,
The finished stone of Forcarthu she left,
And the pillar in Cnamchaill.
Whoever sees it will become blind,
Whoever hears it will become deaf,
And anyone who tries to take a piece of the
Rough spoked wheel will die …
After the woman came from the East,
She gave birth to three sons after hard labour.
She died, the light and lively one.
This urgent, unconcealable news was to be heard.
The names of the sons were of great import …
Muach and Cuma and Doirb the noble.
The crowd … [text missing) …
because it is appropriate that they shall hear it:
That as long as over the stately Banba [Ireland]
The names of the three sons are remembered
As the truthful story tells …

No catastrophe will befall its inhabitants.

The hill where this woman from the East is buried,

To surpass all other women, This is the name it was given:

The Hill of Tlachtga.

These versions of the story are quite likely to be the confusion of two different ones – most likely ecclesiastical fantasy, appearing to be based on a medieval tale of the beheading of John the Baptist, in which *Mog Ruith* takes on the role of executioner. In the *banshenchas* version, *Tlachtga's* story is partly merged with the myth of *Etain* and *Midir*, also the unknown martyr that *Tlachtga* is said to have slain may be a confusion with the account of her father described above. *Mogh Ruith* has three children but the two sons appear to be of no importance, it is *Tlachtga* who is central to the story of the bizarre wheel, stone and pillar that seem to have immense power.

Tlachgta is said to have created a pillar stone called *Cnamhcaill*, meaning 'bone damage', out of a fragment of *Roth Ramach*, her father's wheel. It is said to kill all who touch it, blind those that gaze upon it and deafen those that hear it. This pillar is thought to represent lightning, which would tie in with the meaning of her name, as lightning was likened to a spear thrown at the ground. *Tlachtga* was most likely not only an ancient goddess, discredited and demoted by Christian scribes, but a goddess of the sun and lightning and possibly death and rebirth too.

According to some versions, *Tlachtga* returned to Ireland with her father, bringing the *Roth Ramach* with them and it was seen flying over a *feis* (fayre) at Tara. According to Eugene O'Curry in *Manners and Customs of the Ancient Irish*, the wheel was destroyed at the Battle of Sollyhead in 914 CE, to the west of Tipperary town. The pillar taken from part of the wheel (*Cnamhcaill*) supposedly survives to this day in the townland of Dromline, just outside Tipperary.

Whatever the circumstances of her death actually were, *Tlachtga* is generally agreed to have given birth to three boys – *Doirb*, *Cumma* and *Muach*. Her triple birth and subsequent death symbolises giving her power to the land in the form of her sons, and like *Tailitu* (foster mother of *Lugh*) she gives her name to the place of her death, where she gave birth.

In the oldest version of the story, the three sons became rulers of Munster, Leinster and Connaught (three of the provinces of Ireland). It was said that while their names are remembered Ireland would be safe from invasion by strangers. In later times, as the Celtic royalty and aristocracy decayed, they were indeed forgotten and Ireland, as we all know, fell under control of the English Tudors. So, it becomes clear that *Tlachtga* is intimately linked with the symbolic death and rebirth of the land at *Samhain*; perhaps this is why her story was rewritten to diminish her impact and ensure that she and her sacred temple were forgotten by mainstream society.

MOGH RUITH

The situation is somewhat more complex with the father of *Tlachtga*. Interestingly, *Mogh Ruith* appears to be two or three entirely different characters – the Munster Druid who aided his fellow Munster men in battle against the forces of *Cormac Mac Airt*, who lived sometime around 200 CE and the slave/assistant of Simon Magus around 30 CE or, if we look deeper, the god or mythological person associated with his goddess daughter *Tlachtga*, perhaps 1500–1000 BCE. *Mogh Ruith* is given as one of either the *Tuatha Dé Danann* or their opponents the *Fir Bolg* and some of the poets said that he lived through the reigns of nineteen kings. In *Lebor Gabála Érenn* he is mentioned briefly just once (as *Mug Roith* in Volume V).

He is listed among the fallen of the battle of *Loch Léin*, during the reign of *Conmael*, the 2nd Milesian King of Ireland, perhaps three and a half thousand years ago. Geoffrey Keating's 'General History Of Ireland' dated the reign of *Conmael* from 1239–09 BCE, while the *Annals of the Four Masters* dated it from 1651–21 BCE. His name means 'devotee of the wheel', which probably relates to the sun. In the story *Tlachtga* is credited with creating the wheel *Roth Ramach* or creating it together with her father and also Simon Magus:

> she made the red wheel, greatly-strong,
> together with great and beloved *Mug*
> and with Símón sechtmisid.

A clue in the name 'devotee of the wheel' indicates, to me at least, that the wheel must be primarily associated with *Mogh Ruith* and probably had nothing to do with Simon Magus at all. It seems that some writers draw a comparison between *Mogh Ruith* and the Gaulish god *Taranis*, who carried a wheel (thought to represent the sun) and was a god of thunder and lightning. Is it possible that *Mogh Ruith* is an ancient Irish form of *Taranis*? Given the associations of *Mogh Ruith*'s daughter *Tlachtga* with lightning, this further reinforces the idea of father and daughter being ancient deities of thunder and lightning, possibly with solar associations too.

As for the connection between *Mogh Ruith* and Simon Magus – if Geoffrey Keating was correct in suggesting that Tara, *Uisneach*, *Tailtin* and *Tlachtga* were all constructed around the same time, based on what is now known of Tara, *Uisneach* and *Tailtin*, this would place *Tlachtga* at some time before 1000 BCE.

It is well known that prophet/magician Magus was considered to be a contemporary of Jesus of Nazareth (around 30 CE) in the Middle East, also thought by some to be the Messiah. Given the time period of Simon Magus, it is hard to see how *Tlachtga* (and *Mogh Ruith*) could have been contemporaries – they clearly existed either much earlier or well over a hundred years after Simon Magus. As we explore the tales of *Mogh Ruith*, it is clear that there may well have been two or three characters of the same name, perhaps the later Druid taking his name from a much earlier god?   Whatever the case may be, the likelihood of Magus actually being literally connected to either *Tlachtga* or *Mogh Ruith* is probably zero – I would suggest that a demonising story of *Mogh Ruith* has somehow become conflated with the origin story of *Tlachtga*, leading to a severe corruption of the original story. In the following passages, *Mogh Ruith* is cast as the killer of John the Baptist:

'The Executioner of John the Baptist', from MS 1 of the Scottish Collection:

> Askelon, the royal seat,
> In which the great deed was done;
> There, not lasting was the fame,
> John the noble was slain.

> 'What evil woman among you
> Will take in hand my beheading?
> Not one from east or west,
> Of the blood of Foreigners or Gaels.

> 'Thou handsome yellow-haired John,
> Yonder is a Gael beyond all others;
> His abode is far away in the west,
> In the lands of the western men.'

'I ask a boon from Christ who loves me,'
Said John the noble,
'That no comely Gael may get
Food nor rainment in any case.'

Said *Mogh Ruith* without grace,
'Give to me even his rainment,
And I shall cut off his head
For the weal of the men of Ireland.'

Then was John beheaded,
The Gael will suffer therefrom;
Much silver and gold
Was put under the head east in Askelon.

And again:

Book of Leinster: 144 a50, translated by Erik Stogellou:

The time of nineteen kings successively lasted the live
Of Mog Ruith in battle:
From Ruth mc. Rigo – whose fame enormous –
to the angry raging Cairpri Liphechar.

A tree branch in the Alpine mountains to cut down
For the cows of Simon in the snow,
this is what broke his one great eye.
Ten years he spent with Simon.

There is another bizarre excerpt from the *Book of Ballymote*, which explains how *Mogh Ruith* loses an eye while a student of Simon Magus and later the other, becoming totally blind. This story unites *Mogh Ruith* of the Simon Magus stories with the *Mogh Ruith*, Druid of Valentia Island, despite the obvious time difference of at least 150 years! Note also that there is no mention at all of *Tlachtga*, who is generally to be found in the story along with Simon Magus and her father.

'The Adventures of *Mogh Ruith*' (*Imtheachta Moighi Ruith*) from the *Book of Ballymote*, 265 b65 and YBL 190 a10, translated by Erik Stohellou:

> Here are the adventures of *Mog Ruith*:
> *Cacht*, the daughter of *Catmand* of the Briton in the Isle of Man. Her mother was taken over into captivity. The number of 50 girls has been spread over Ireland. *Cacht* was brought in the house of the *Roth mac Righuill*, king of Ireland; and there she was in constant servitude and slavery. A wise man stayed with the king, viz *Cuindeasg mac Fhirglain* from the tribe of *Fergus mac Rossa* of Ulster. *Cuindeasg* caused that the slave girl became pregnant by him. The night *Cacht* lay in, said the Druid, that the name the son, who was born in the night, would be heard about Ireland and famous. *Roth* said: 'My name is the one he will have.' Therefore, it was the name given to *Mog Ruith*. He has now been raised and dealt with the King with the science and became a sage. He found the teaching over there and went to *Scathach*, a war Woman, to learn the profession of arms, until he was a master.
>
> A Druid over there said to him: 'If the Druid art would be that you learned today, your name would be on all Ireland.' – 'I will learn it,' said *Mog Ruith*. He learned, so that he was a (famous)

Sage in Ireland. He then went to the druid Simon, to learn with him. And he had left his wife pregnant in *Darbrui*, viz *Dron*, daughter of *Oengus mac Echach Lairen* (and her son) viz *Buan*, and it was of (her son) *Fercorp*, that his wife was pregnant. *Mog Ruith* spent thirty-three years near Simon. Then he mutilated one of his eyes when he was killing a calf in great snow in the Alps mountains. And the other eye was blinded when he was holding the sun for two days in *Darbri*, so that he made two days to one. Of which he mutilated one of his eyes (= the other), so that he was blind.

Then he came to Ireland (and went) until he reached *Dairbriu*. He (had) a boy with him. (The boy) looked into the house from the rear. *Mog Ruith* asked: 'What is the woman doing?' – 'She sits in the chair and a handsome young man with her. And they are friendly with each other,' said the lad. 'Bring me the ax,' said *Mog Ruith*. 'I will carry out the ax,' said the boy, 'if everyone is asleep.' He was (on the point) to kill his own son. However, they waited patiently for three days and three nights. On the last night asked *Mog Ruith*: 'How are they doing here,' he asked, he answered him. 'Thirty-three years (have passed),' they say, 'until tonight, since our father went of us. Not until then he was looking for (our) community. As for me and my mother, she went they never with a man, and I took no wife.' He went then and approached the fire. The woman recognised him now and its limbs, and she put a robe around him. He was the High-druide of all Ireland at that time, and so he it is *Fiachra Muillethan mac Eogain* and Munster People asked for advice at the siege of *Drom Damgaire*.

Finally, we come to the epic account of *Mogh Ruith*, the great Druid, aiding King *Fiachra Muilleathan* and the men of Munster in their battle against High King *Cormac Mac Airt*. This fantastical account demonstrates the immense powers of *Mogh Ruith*. Although it does not mention Simon Magus/sechtmisid or *Tlachtga*, there is a brief mention of 'Simon's stone' and 'Simon's tinderbox', presumably objects that once belonged to Simon Magus.

'The Siege of Knocklong' from the *Book of Lismore*, translated by *Seán Ó Duinn*:

'Where is the magic of the south? How is it that you cannot help us in this appalling situation?' 'We haven't succeeded ...' said *Dil*. 'No,' said *Fiacha*, 'if you had provided water only, we would never have conceded the tribute – not as long as one person remained alive in the province. Do you know of anybody in the area who could help?' 'No,' said *Dil*, 'except perhaps for your own teacher *Mogh Roith*, for it is with his aid that I fostered you. Moreover, it was he who made the prediction on the day of your birth that the siege by *Leath Choinn* which you are under today would take place. If *Mogh Roith* cannot help you nobody can, for *Mogh Roith* spent his first seven years occult training in *Sí Charn Breachnatan* under the direction of the druidess *Banbhuana*, the daughter of *Deargdhualach*. Neither inside nor outside of the sí dwelling place nor in any other place is to be found a form of magic which he has not practised, and among the Men of Ireland, *Mogh Roith* is the only one who ever learned the magic arts within a sí. However, he would do nothing without a large recompense, for he has no interest in your predicament, nor in your status, and you, for your part, have paid little attention to him.'

By means of a magical fire of rowan wood, *Mogh Ruith* attacks *Cormac's* forces, ending with a spectacular blood rain on his royal encampment:

Mogh Roith then shot a druidic breath into the air and the firmament so that an obscuring thicket and a dark cloud arose over *Ceann Cláire* and from it descended a shower of blood, and *Mogh Roith* began to chant a spell:

I cast a spell,
on the power of cloud,
may there be a rain
of blood on grass,
let it be throughout the land,
a burning of the crowd,
may there be a trembling
on the warriors of *Conn*.

On the completion of this rhetoric the cloud moved on until it was above *Ceann Cláire*; from that it moved on again until it was above *Cormac's* camp and then proceeded to Tara.

Finally, there is a relatively modern and rather strange folk story of the death of *Mogh Ruith*, which is at the hands of the *Cailleach* (the hag of the Beara Peninsula), who reputedly periodically in a state of decrepitude returned to the sea to regenerate herself, and in becoming young again secures a new husband. In the story, the one she ensnares is none other than the Druid *Mogh Ruith* of Valentia Island:

Now, before the marriage the Druid had an eye for the witch's sister, but the hag, being a woman of a jealous disposition and having the power of the occult, cast a spell on the Druid, and lured him into marriage with herself. That was grand, as far as it went, but one day, didn't the old charm slip, and the man realised that he had been conned into marrying the wrong woman … and off he went cavorting with the sister. Not the best move in the world, I can tell you, for when the auld hag discovered what was afoot, there was a fury on her. Nothing would satisfy her till she had it out with your man. She ranted and raved like a *bean sí*, and next thing she took off after him. Let me tell you, himself didn't hang around. Given the knowledge that he was in imminent danger, the man took to his heels and made straight for the River Funchion. Well if he did, the hag was after him like a March hare. Down the hill *Mogh Ruith* bounded, and the wife in hot pursuit. Twas a sight to behold, the two of them. She was fast, but let me tell you, he was faster and being fleet of foot *Mogh Ruith* reached the river first and he was half way across when the wife arrived on. There was a steam on her and her puffing and panting, but begorra she assessed her situation well, and there and then she lifted up a boulder the size of a meteor, and she flung it with all her might at your man. Down he went like a stone, pinned to the bottom of the river, and try as he might there was no return for the poor man. There he stopped until the last remaining breath passed from him.

The above story is from labbacallee.weebly.com. The River Funshion flows close by Labbacallee, in Co. Cork and various versions of this story exist, including one by a local historian Christie Roche. You can listen to his discussion of it in conversation with Del Richardson at youtube.com/watch?v=tpnjDrKUQBg.

So from the ancient literature we can see there is a lot of confusion regarding both *Tlachtga* and *Mogh Ruith*, especially the latter. From my reading of the texts, I believe, like some other commentators (most notably John Gilroy and Daithi O'Hogan), that they were both ancient gods. It is possible that the Munster Druid of the third century CE was named so after the ancient *Mogh Ruith*, or it could be a copying mistake that has been carried forward down the centuries, or a merger of an unknown person with the ancient character of *Mogh Ruith*. Without further material to clarify the matter, this is all just speculation and cannot be proven one way or the other.

What is very clear is that the Christian monks did their best to disparage both *Tlachtga* and *Mogh Ruith*, with *Mogh Ruith* being cast a terrible villain, responsible for the death of John the Baptist and using the *Roth Ramach* as a weapon of terror. Such tactics, to discredit pagan practices, deities and personages, were common in a country that barely conformed to the norms of Christianity well into the second millennium. Even today, one can hear it said that if you scratch an Irish Christian you find the pagan lurking just under the surface!

The Catholic Church constantly attempted to stamp out lingering pagan customs, including creating hysterical propaganda, but with little real success. Christian scribes envisage the *Roth Ramach* as a terrible machine of destructive power that would fly overhead on Judgement Day to punish sinners. It is recorded that there was a panic in 1096 when it had been prophesised that the flying wheel would pass over Ireland bringing death and destruction to two-thirds of the population as retribution for *Mogh Ruith* having killed John the Baptist. As a result of this prediction, the Bishop of Dublin ordered several days of penance and prayer to prevent the looming disaster.

It is clear is that *Tlachtga* was important enough that the main centre of Irish Druids and the start point of *Samhain* celebrations was named after her. Despite the negative view of both her and her father, their story, albeit probably grossly distorted, has been preserved in the literature.

Despite the Church's best efforts, the traditions of *Samhain* survived as *Oíche Shamhna* or Halloween. Although they failed to erase traditions of *Samhain* and the other seasonal festivals, they did succeed in making sure that the general population would forget both *Tlachtga* and the sacred site named after her.

Aerial view of the Tlachtga site at the Hill Of Ward, as it is today.

CHAPTER 4

Tlachtga – the Sacred Site

The Hill of Ward, also known as *Tlachtga*, lies less than 10 miles south-west of Teltown, approximately 12 miles west of Tara, perhaps Ireland's most famous ancient site. It is also about 10 miles south of Loughcrew and about 18 miles south-west of Newgrange, another world famous and important ancient site.

In the immediate vicinity of *Tlachtga* are several ancient sites, largely unknown but still of interest. To the west of the Hill of Ward lies the small town of Athboy; in the town park called Fair Green lies Fairgreen ringfort. This *ráth* of unknown age is quite small and the walls are completely erased, leaving just a raised platform that has around ten trees of various sizes growing on it.

To the south-east of the Hill of Ward only half a kilometre away lie the scant remains of *Timpeal Cuimhneas*, an early Christian settlement said to have been established by St Patrick, which is now a disused graveyard. Also about half a kilometre from the main site, to the south, lies *An Tobar Druí*, the Druids' Well, also known as Coffey's Well. This well lies on private farm land and it is quite sizeable, about 2.5m wide. It has some very small steps down to the water level, but the well has been badly neglected and is currently in need of repair work. There are two other wells on or near the main road from Athboy, but these are far more recent. One of these is near Rathmore Castle (over 1.5km to the north-west) and dedicated to St Lawrence. Rathmore Castle was built by the Normans in the fourteenth century on the site of a much older ringfort, which was reputedly the home of *Niall Glun Dubh* (Niall of the black knee), recorded as High King of Ireland in 916–19 CE.

To the south-east near a sixteenth-century church lies the third well, Tobairnaglass (*Tobar na Glas*), which translates roughly as 'the green well'. As far as can be ascertained, *An Tobar Druí* is the original well that serviced *Tlachtga* and it was built in a style typical of truly ancient wells. It is certainly far more ancient than the other two in the vicinity of *Tlachtga*.

Also not far from *Tlachtga* are supposedly the remains of a *Teach Allais* or 'sweat house/lodge'. These were heated using turf fires and after emptying were used as steam baths, with water thrown on the hot walls to create steam and herbs also used. Some lodges remained in use into the nineteenth century. It is impossible for me to guess how ancient this medicinal/ritual stone hut was, as its exact location is unknown to myself or anyone that I have asked about it.

In 1953 there was an amazing treasure find at Dressogue, a townland 1km east of *Tlachtga*, which was ploughed up by a farmer. The golden hoard discovered consisted of a gold pin and three gold bracelets. The bracelets (now in the National Museum of Ireland) were dated to around 650–250 BCE, the late Bronze Age, and the pin was dated as 400–200 BCE.

In addition to the places already mentioned, according to Gilroy, the remains of a total of sixteen ringforts are to be found in the area surrounding *Tlachtga*, which further demonstrates that this was once a place of no small importance.

LOCATION

Various authors have speculated about why this hill was chosen to create this series of four circular ditches and the barrow mound in its centre, which is around 150m in diameter. We cannot possibly have a complete answer to that question, however, one major factor may be that it is visible from the Hill of Tara and at 119m it is the highest point in the locality. One theory for its location is the ease of delivery of the sacred flame/fire to Tara. It has been suggested by many that travelling by boat was far easier than travelling by land in ancient Ireland, because of the extensive forest cover slowing progress.

Some speculate that the sacred flame was lit at the extinct volcano of Lambay Island and brought westward up the River Boyne to *Tlachtga*. It is fairly certain that the fire at *Tlachtga* was lit before that of Tara and quite possibly the flame was brought to Tara to light the fire of the High King. To the west of *Tlachtga* is a small river (Tremblertown/ Yellowford), which runs down the hill towards the River Boyne. This famous river runs slightly north-west of Tara, but at one time it is thought the River Gabhra (meaning White Mare), connected to the Boyne, ran closer to Tara. If this was the case, it may well have been easier to bring a contained fire or flaming torch from *Tlachtga* to Tara by boat. Sadly, we are unlikely to ever find evidence that proves that this was the case, but logically, there is a good argument to suggest that is possibly what happened during the pre-Christian order, that of the Druids.

Tobar an Druí, the original Druid's Well, just to the south of the Hill of Ward.

TLACHTGA – THE SITE

The series of circular ditches has been damaged over the centuries but must have been an impressive sight in its day. It's quite likely that the outer ring would have had a wooden palisade, like most ringforts would have done. It's also possible that there was a wooden hut or structure in the centre, although this is mere speculation as the site may not have been permanently occupied. There is nothing to suggest that anyone actually lived on the site, but it is likely that people lived very close by. Local tradition is that the Druids and elites of the local society (tribe) would have lived close to the site and the ordinary people lived further down the hill. Certainly the gold hoard, which would have belonged to important people, was found a very short distance from *Tlachtga*.

As this is thought to be the main centre of the Druids, like Tara (where people came to see the *Ard Rí*, or High King, from all over Ireland), the Druids of Ireland most likely congregated at *Tlachtga*. If Tara was the place of sovereignty and kings, *Tlachtga* was the place of religion, magic and the Druids. The chief Druid, who served the king, was called an *Olamh*, as were all Druids of the highest position; below the *Druí/Draoi* there were *Fáidh* (shaman/healer) and *File* (bards). If indeed this was the main centre of Druidry in Ireland, they would have gathered from across the country at important times, perhaps before the gatherings at Tara. None of the practical details of what the Druids did and how they organised their meetings, or when, has been recorded – what we know of their ideas, poems, satires, spells, divination, etc. is all fragmentary, described as small parts of a much larger story.

One must wonder who built the site and when? This remains a mystery, without the help of modern archaeology (more on that later). We do know that Ireland was not composed of just one people – there were at least four waves of invaders in ancient times. The early invaders are called

the *Chriutni* and little is known of them. A later group, the *Erainn*, are
thought to be Celts arriving around 500 BCE or so, some of whom settled
in Co. Meath (where *Tlachtga* and Tara are located). The *Ebdani/Eblani/
Blanii* tribes are thought to have settled in Meath but one of the tribes that
settled in the area of Tara were the *Luigni*, who traditionally protected the
king – sometimes called the Old Tribe of Tara (*Sentuatha Tramach*).

Before the Norman Conquest there were four provinces but around
nine kingdoms, each of which were split up into clans, most of whom were
in frequent conflict with their neighbours. Throughout Irish history and
in the run-up to the Norman invasion of 1169, there were near-constant
wars between provinces or between sub-kingdoms, and even between the
High King and provincial kings. As a result of this frequent warfare we
see developments end and begin again at different time periods.

In Newman's *Tara, An Archaeological Survey*, he suggests that there were
five ancient roads leading out from Tara, featuring Petrie's 1839 map. It
has been suggested that the faint line of an ancient road can be detected in
the landscape, in very dry weather, running south from *Tlachtga* towards
Tara, although no firm archaeological evidence has been found of this or
any of the five roads described. What is certain is that the Hill of Ward
(*Tlachtga*) can be seen on the horizon from Tara, so it is likely that a
substantial fire lit there could be viewed and likewise a fire on Tara could
be seen from *Tlachtga*.

There has been massive speculation about the connection between
Tlachtga and Tara – processions by road, delivery of the sacred fire/flame
by boat, and about the exact purpose of *Tlachtga* and the role the Druids
played there and in the assemblies at Tara. John Gilroy goes into great
detail in this regard, which unfortunately cannot be substantiated. One
can assume correctly that there is a deep connection between the two
places, running back into the first millennium BCE and continuing until
the end of the pagan era, but we have very little to go on in the way of

specifics. Accounts exist of feasting at Tara and also of the *Feis Tramach*, or Festival of Tara, that involved the ritual marriage of the king with the land, a symbol of the goddess of the land bestowing authority and sovereignty on the king. However, we have no accounts (at least not translated) of rituals performed on *Samhain* at Tara or anywhere else.

DECLINE INTO DISUSE

We know that by the death of St Patrick, Christianity had become quite well established in Ireland (around 461 CE), although it took longer than is generally acknowledged for it to become dominant and displace paganism completely. It is generally accepted that *Colm Cille* (St Columba) was a Druid in 521 CE before he was baptised into Christianity. *Breandán* (St Brendan), born in 484 CE and famous for his voyage into the west, is said to have founded the holy well on Valentia Island. In local tradition it is believed that St Brendan sailed to Valentia across Dingle Bay and climbed the cliffs near Culloo, arriving just in time to baptise and anoint two dying pagans. It is called *Tobar Olla Bhreanain*, the well of St Brendan's anointing.

Having visited the site myself, I concluded that the original well is extremely ancient and the edifice built on top of it is relatively recent. In addition to the large stone crosses at the site are some huge stones very close by (20–30m away), but none are to be found anywhere else nearby. It is highly likely that this site was in use long before St Brendan arrived on the island to convert the pagans – as with many of the Christian stories, they are a means of appropriating the places and cultural symbols of the long-established pagan order. I personally believe this legend of St Brendan's Well, like many others, is pure invention to dismiss or denigrate the older religion.

Both these examples prove that Druidry and the old pagan order was still in existence almost 100 years after St Patrick first preached in Ireland. In addition to this, the existence of pagan-style graves and graveyards, long after St Patrick died, proves that paganism continued to exist. Christian burials were in a different style to pagan burials and did not include grave goods. They were generally in an east–west direction and did not involve the earlier cist burial or burial mounds.

Excavations at Caherconnell in Co. Clare, Ireland, have shown both pagan and Christian practices in the same location. These findings prove that Celtic paganism was not so quick to die out. The discovery was made by the Caherconnell Archaeology Field School. The results of radiocarbon dating of the bodies of a woman and two babies have revealed that the human remains date from the second half of the sixth century CE to the first half of the seventh. This places them well within the chronological bounds of what was once termed 'Early Christian Ireland'. Further examples cited by Tiernan McGarry could imply that pagan burials, although in rapid decline, continued into the eighth century.

From this information, we might conclude that *Tlachtga* was probably not immediately abandoned after St Patrick brought Christianity to Tara. Despite the presence of *Timpeal Cuimhneas*, built in the fifth century, only 500m away from the hill, this does not mean that *Tlachtga* was entirely replaced. The site south-east of *Tlachtga* is tiny and could not have housed more than a handful of people, while *Tlachtga,* at 150m in diameter, remained a huge site, probably in use for some significant amount of time to come.

Tlachtga may have ceased to be a Druidic site within a century of the arrival of Christianity, but this cannot be proven. However, we do know that it continued to be an important site for assemblies. According to the *Annals of the Four Masters*, it was burned to the ground in 903 CE by the

O'Neills of Tyrone (in Northern Ireland), which implies that buildings still existed at the site at that point in time.

Sometime after, *Tlachtga* was also attacked by the Vikings. Viking attacks on Ireland reputedly began in 795 CE with coastal raids, but eventually they settled areas such as Dublin, Cork, Wexford, Waterford and Limerick, with easy access to the sea. Attempts by the Vikings (and Leinstermen) to take over Ireland were thwarted by High King Brian Boru (*Brian Bóruma mac Cennétig*) in 1014, but at huge cost – resulting in his death and the death of his son (*Murchad*) and grandson (*Toirdelbach*). Huge numbers of nobility on both sides died, eliminating many of the royal bloodlines of Ireland completely.

Despite their defeat, the Vikings continued to attack the Irish and the High King (from Meath) Mallachy II. After erasing historic Kells as well as Duleek and Clonard, they proceeded to *Tlachtga*, where they engaged the forces of Malachy. The battle, fought just below the brow of the hill, did not go well for the Vikings and they were routed.

Tlachtga appears on record again in 1167. By this time, after the changing hands of the High Kingship between several dynasties, it had come to Rory O'Connor (*Ruaidrí mac Tairrdelbach Ua Conchobair*) in 1166. As part of his feud with Dermot MacMorrough (*Diarmaid mac Murchadha*), the King of Leinster, Rory invaded Leinster and banished Dermot.

Dermot fled to Britain and then sought out the Norman king (Henry II) in France, looking for support to take back his kingdom. With war and unrest still plaguing Ireland, O'Connor held an assembly (*aonach*) at *Tlachtga* in 1167, bringing together the kings of *Oriel* (Louth), *Breifney* (Leitrim/Cavan), *Ulidi* (Ulster province) and the Vikings (from Dublin). In total, there were 13,000 horsemen present, plus attendants and foot soldiers.

The assembly was joined by the Archbishop of Dublin, Lawrence O'Toole, no doubt fulfilling the function of arbiter and negotiator that would formally have be undertaken by a high-ranking Druid in former times. The annals record that, 'they passed a good many resolutions and separated in peace and amity, without battle or controversy'.

O'Connor presumably was keen to restore peace at *Tlachtga*, not least because of the threat of the impending return of Dermot MacMorrough with new allies. However, his attempts to prepare for an invasion bore little fruit – the Norman invasion of 1169 proved how easily they (with Flemish mercenary and Leinstermen's help) could defeat the Irish in battle. Henry II, to consolidate the first success, launched a second and much larger invasion himself in 1171 to ensure his control over his new subjects. MacMorrough was killed in May 1171 and failed to profit from his alliance. Ferns (his capital) was completely destroyed, although his castle still stands today, albeit half ruined.

Henry accepted the submission of the Irish kings and the High King (Rory O'Connor) in Dublin in November 1171, ensuring his moral claim to Ireland, granted by the supposed 1155 papal bull *Laudabiliter*, which was reconfirmed in 1172 by Pope Alexander III, and by a synod of all the Irish bishops at the Synod of Cashel (also in 1172). Henry II became 'Lord of Ireland', but before he could consolidate his new Lordship, he had to go to France to deal with the rebellion of his wife (Eleanor of Aquitaine) and three of his sons in 1173. He never returned to Ireland. Incidentally, O'Connor abdicated as the last High King of Ireland in 1183 and also abdicated as King of Connacht in 1186.

In 1171 Henry had granted lands in North Leinster to Hugh De Lacy, to thwart the ambitions of Richard De Clare (the famous Strongbow of 1169). De Lacy consolidated his position and dealt with troublesome minor kings and chieftains who resisted the Norman advance. The King of *Breffini*, Tiernan O'Rourke, was one such troublesome Irish chieftain, who De Lacy arranged to meet at *Tlachtga* for a negotiation in 1172. The two men were supposed to meet alone, but Tiernan's rival Donal

O'Rourke arrived with De Lacy and, producing an axe, killed Tiernan while receiving a fatal wound himself. De Lacy decapitated Tiernan and had the body brought to Dublin for public display as a warning to would-be rebels.

With *Tlachtga* firmly in the hands of the Normans, it became part of a Norman manor, which was centred on Athboy, where a castle was built and another one to the north at Rathmore.

From this point onwards there is little reference to *Tlachtga* until the Cromwellian invasion of Ireland. It is tradition that Oliver Crowell and his forces camped on *Tlachtga*, overlooking Rathmore Castle. Some of the damage to the site of *Tlachgta* is attributed to Cromwell and his forces – perhaps using the ditches for target practice or digging them in part to create new ramparts for themselves.

The Plunkets, who still occupied the castle, were commanded to appear before Cromwell to answer accusations of involvement in rebellion. When Christopher Plunket and his eleven sons rode up the hill to the English encampment they were met with cannon fire, echoing the earlier treachery of Hugh De Lacy. All of the Plunkets were killed and Lady Plunket, who was observing from the tower of the castle, either fell or threw herself to her death.

It appears that the Plunkets' lands were confiscated and granted to John Bligh, one of the Cromwellian opportunists who had come to Ireland seeking his fortune. Bligh took over Rathmore Castle and his family became ennobled as the Earls of Darnley in 1738, keeping hold of the castle and the surrounding lands until 1909. However, *Tlachtga* itself became owned by the Ward family in the seventeenth century and thereafter became known as the Hill of Ward.

ARCHAEOLOGICAL EXPLORATION

Renewed interest in *Tlachtga*, perhaps instigated by the revival of the celebrations in 1999, led to calls for a proper archaeological survey of this ancient historical site. Treasa Kerrigan, a Master in Archaeology at UCD, archaeologist and pagan priestess, first visited *Tlachtga* in 2012. She also visited the archaeological dig in 2014 and participated in another two years later. She concurred with others that interest in the hill dramatically increased following John Gilroy's book, and subsequently politician David Gilroy's involvement added to this.

In 2012 the Hill of Ward Archaeological Project was funded by the Heritage Council and the Office for Public Works to perform a geophysical survey at the Hill of Ward and a number of localities in the immediate area (the embanked enclosure, Wardstown deserted settlement, the northern enclosure banks). This was undertaken in collaboration with Dr Chris Carey, formerly of the Universities of Exeter and Birmingham, his field assistant Hannah Ventre and a number of volunteers from the School of Archaeology, UCD, who found previously unidentified features such as outer banks, an embanked enclosure near *Timpeal Cuimhneas* and a possible settlement south-east of the hilltop site.

2014 DIG

Dr Steve Davis led the archaeological survey and digs in both 2014 and 2016. A research excavation was carried over three weeks in May and June 2014 at *Tlachtga*, jointly funded by the Royal Irish Academy, the Office of Public Works and Meath County Council. The project was led by Dr Davis of the School of Archaeology, UCD, and the excavation was directed by Caitríona Moore. Three trenches and three test pits were excavated in 2014, and a further two trenches in 2015 consisting of Sondages 1 and 2, selected based on data collected in the 2012 survey and further explorations of the site. The details of the digs were published, as described by Moore and Davis:

> Geophysical survey and LiDAR data in the vicinity of the site have identified several previously unrecorded monuments, amongst which are a very large tri- or quadrivallate enclosure underlying the present upstanding monument, and a small enclosure to the south, partially overlapping the present monument. The programme of excavation focused on establishing chronological control on these features and investigating a small section of the outermost embankment of the upstanding monument, with the principal aim of understanding the sequence of construction at the site. Three trenches and three test pits were excavated.

Trench 1

Trench 1 was half-sectioned lengthwise and the western half was excavated. Subsequently, due to time constraints, the remaining in situ deposits were half-sectioned crosswise and the southern half were excavated. With 75% of the deposits being excavated. Four layers of charcoal were found in this trench, as well as a coin (from topsoil), pieces of worked and possibly worked chert and flint and a piece of sandstone which has a series of four parallel grooves picked into its surface, reminiscent of megalithic art, and there is a strong possibility that this stone is part of a larger object.

Trench 2

Trench 2 measured 10m × 3m and was located to the north-west of the upstanding monument. It was positioned to investigate the innermost ditch of the earlier trivallate enclosure of which there are no visible surface remains. As well as bone fragments and charcoal flecks, a piece of cattle bone from was found that has been radiocarbon dated to the fourth century BCE. Finds from trench two comprised a fragment of a bone pin from the final ditch fill, and four objects, a small metal disc, a clay pipe stem, a possible chert flake and a piece of worked flint, from topsoil.

Trench 3

Trench 3 measured 8m × 3m and was located to the south of the upstanding monument. It was positioned to investigate the ditch of a small (*c.* 30m in diameter) circular enclosure of which there are no visible surface remains. At the south-west end of the trench was a shallow linear feature containing a sterile fill of moderately compact brown silty clay. Close to it were three post-holes filled with deposits of clay, stones and charcoal. Hazel charcoal from one of these has been dated to between the twelfth and tenth centuries BCE.

Towards the north-east end of trench three was a rock-cut ditch which measured 3.05m wide and 0.8m deep. The primary fill of the ditch was moderately compact silty clay with frequent inclusions of stone and a moderate amount of well-preserved animal bone. Several large pieces of cattle bone were also seemingly placed at intervals at the base of the fill directly on bedrock. One of these has been radiocarbon dated to the fifth century CE.

In the north-east corner of the exposed section of ditch was a juvenile burial. This lay in a small deposit of silty clay and was covered with several medium to large flat stones. Adjacent to the lower part of the skeleton were a number of upright smaller stones. The burial was orientated along the width of the ditch (north-east/south-west) with the head and torso resting directly on the bedrock and the pelvis and legs on the clay fill. It seems likely that the clay fill was intentionally used to cover the burial before the larger stones were put in place. Examination has indicated that the remains are those of a child of 3–5 months old and the remains have been radiocarbon dated to the fifth century CE.

Test Pits 1–3

Test pit 1, to the east of Trench 3 exposed a shallow linear feature with sterile clay fill which produced a piece of worked flint and a piece of quartz. Like the linear feature exposed within trench 3, this may be a relatively modern agricultural feature. Test pit 2 in the centre of the upstanding monument uncovered part of what may be a large pit the upper fill of which appeared to be re-deposited topsoil, stone and large amounts of animal bone. Beneath these were stratified hearth deposits consisting of layers of burnt clay, charcoal and the remains of an *in situ* burnt timber (oak) and post. A fragment of the timber has been dated to between the eleventh and thirteenth centuries CE. Finds from Test pit 2 included a piece of polished bone, possibly worked flint and chert, a fragment of a possible rubbing stone and an unidentified metal object from topsoil. The base of the archaeological deposits in Test pit 2 was not reached due to the depth of the material and issues of health and safety. Test pit 3 to the north of Trench 1 contained no features of archaeological significance.

2015 DIG

The Hill of Ward geophysical and LiDAR survey in the vicinity of the site have identified several previously unrecorded monuments, amongst which are a very large closely-spaced trivallate enclosure, partially underlying the present upstanding monument, and a small enclosure to the south, partially intercut with the present monument. In 2015 two trenches were excavated to investigate these monuments.

Trench 4

Trench 4 measured 30m × 5m and was located to the south-east of the upstanding monument placed to extend from outside the third ditch section through to the interior of the monument, stopping short of the present monument of *Tlachtga*. Removal of sod and topsoil revealed a small ground stone axe and finds of chert, flint, metal and ceramic. At the southern end of Trench 4 adjacent to the limit of excavation was an oval pit. Approximately 2m north of this was the outermost ditch of the trivallate enclosure. A human lower mandible fragment was recovered from the basal fill and possible lithics and pieces of worked bone were found in all fills.

Towards the centre of Trench 4 was the middle ditch of the trivallate enclosure. The primary fill of the ditch comprised soft, silty clay with frequent pieces of shattered limestone and occasional flecks of charcoal and pieces of animal bone. This was probably deliberately backfilled bank material and included a bone spindle whorl. The inner ditch of the trivallate enclosure lay 4m north of the middle ditch. It comprised a very large rock-cut ditch with a roughly U-shaped profile measuring 1.44–2.16m wide at the base increasing to 3.4m at the top, and 1.26m deep. The primary fill of the ditch was a deep deposit of grey/brown silty clay with very frequent inclusions of shattered stone. Finds included a single human molar, possibly worked flint and animal bone. There were three metalled surfaces in trench 4 suggesting that perhaps metalling was once more extensive. A staggered line of stake-holes along the inner edge of the ditch suggests the presence of a wattle wall and various post holes were found.

Trench 5

Trench 5 measured 7.8m × 5m and was orientated north-north-east/south-south-west, placed to investigate the junction of the small southern enclosure and the second from outermost bank and ditch of the upstanding monument of *Tlachtga*. It established conclusively that the ditch of the southern enclosure predates that of the monument. Due to time constraints two large box-sections were excavated at either side of the trench leaving a central baulk. These were numbered Sondage 1 and Sondage 2 and lay respectively to the east and west sides of the trench. Removing the grass and topsoil in Trench 5 produced finds of stone and ceramic. A large fragment of animal bone was found in this deposit, lying directly on the base of the ditch. This is the same as the pattern of deposition seen here in 2014 and demonstrates that placing of animal bone at the base of the ditch was a deliberate act of deposition.

The earliest fill contained a significant amount of animal bone and within Sondage 1 several large fragments were found lying, seemingly placed, on the rock base of the ditch, echoing the deposition of bone within the southern enclosure. The radiocarbon dates obtained in 2014 for these two ditches fall within the same 2-sigma range of 390–540 CE indicating a maximum of a 150-year gap between the construction of the southern enclosure and the second from outermost *Tlachtga* ditch.

Truncating the upper fill of the *Tlachtga* ditch was an irregular cut measuring L 3m min; W 1.1m min.; D 0.12m, within which was a stony deposit. This formed a bse, possibly a crude platform, for a small hearth within which were three layers of charcoal and burnt clay with a combined depth of 0.17m. The presence of the small pit and the two stake-holes all sealed by the uppermost hearth layer suggests it had several phases of activity. This may have been with a relatively short time and appears to have been for some industrial purpose.

Further excavations began in 2016 but were not completed due to health and safety issues, but it is hoped that the UCD team will return again to complete their work, sometime in the future.

SUMMARY OF THE ARCHAEOLOGY

More sites of interest exist at and around the main site of *Tlachtga* than originally thought. Excavations at the *Tlachtga* barrow have revealed that the site was used for millennia, definitely as early as the twelfth century

BCE, if not earlier. There are actually three enclosures now recognised at the site, two of which are no longer visible. A fox tooth recovered from one of the ditches was radiocarbon dated to the fifth century CE.

Trench 1 produced worked chert, and a fragment of a megalithic sandstone featuring four parallel grooves were found, as well as animal bone flakes.

Trench 2 produced part of a bone pin, a small metal disc, a clay pipe stem, a possible chert flake and a piece of worked flint.

Trench 3 produced hazel charcoal dated to between the twelfth to tenth centuries BCE, well-preserved animal bone dated to the fifth century CE, an infant (probably female) burial (three to five months old), surrounded by flat stones, also dated to the fifth century.

Trench 4 produced a small ground stone axe and finds of chert, flint, metal and ceramic, a human lower mandible fragment, charcoal, possible lithics and pieces of worked bone, a bone spindle whorl, a single human molar, possibly worked flint and three metalled evidence of a wattle wall and various post holes.

Trench 5 produced finds of stone and ceramic, a large fragment of animal bone was found in and a significant amount of animal bone dated to 390–540 BCE.

An earlier enclosure was constructed to the south of the main earthworks, but with no more than a 150-year gap between the construction of the southern enclosure and outermost *Tlachtga* ditch. It is most likely that the builders of the ditches were aware of the earlier settlement.

It is clear that there were several phases at *Tlachtga*, a settlement predating the construction of the main site – slightly to the south. The main site was definitely in use around the twelfth to the tenth century BCE. More construction occurred around the sixth to the fourth century BCE. The final phase of construction, the barrow where the infant was found, dates to around the fifth century CE.

The *Tlachtga*/Hill of Ward archaeological dig featured on BBC's archaeological documentary *Digging for Ireland*. Treasa Kerrigan of Sacred Sites provided exclusive footage of the excavation of the infant skeleton, which was included in the TV programme.

Obviously the archaeology is not complete, but it would appear that the speculation about ancient human burials at *Tlachtga* are incorrect – the child buried there is from the late pagan period/early Christian period (fifth century CE), although it shows signs of being a pagan-style burial. The time period at which the site was in a major use began in the late Bronze Age/early Iron Age, which lends weight to an early creation of the *Tlachtga* and *Mogh Ruith* mythology that most likely never involved Simon Magus (biblical first-century CE Samaritan sorcerer). In all likelihood, the original pagan mythology was transformed into a disparaging pseudo-history sometime after the infant burial, in or after the fifth century CE. The archaeological evidence does confirm that *Tlachtga* is an ancient site and is at least 3,000 years old, but a lot of questions remain unanswered. Hopefully further excavations will throw further light on the history of this place.

LOCAL TRADITIONS AT *TLACHTGA*

Academic Michelle Alú was able to talk extensively with local woman Máiréad Byrd (2019) and recorded what she had to say. Her conversation revealed a host of information about the area, including ghostly encounters and stories related to *Tlachtga*. Máiréad has lived in the townland *Rath Cairn* all her life, which is at the bottom of *Tlachtga* hill, to the east. Michelle could see that Máiréad had felt a deep connection and fascination with the hill since childhood, so much so that she and her late husband bought a plot of land and built their family home in a field across from the bottom of the hill during the 1970s. Máiréad recounted how the hill looked when she was a young girl:

When I was small, I would go up there and it was in pristine condition, and there was nothing on it but grass. And it was kept down. There were men there with scythes, and the fort rings were far more spectacular. They were much bigger, you could really like, see the visual impact of a wall, they were just covered, they were covered with grass. But they were very visual, and you really knew … no one ever told you, but you just knew that they were really very important.

Máiréad recalled additional ringforts in two adjoining fields long before the roads were built. They have been ploughed through over the years and ever since then. Unfortunately, there is now nothing left to be seen of them, only the farmers' crops. Máiréad went on to talk about Halloween:

Now, what I would do at Halloween, I would just … on my own, now, I don't mind at night, I think that's all lovely, that's fine [talking about the *Samhain* festival of fire], what I would do on Halloween is, I'd bring my candle and I light my candle, and I would never bring one of those false candles, and I bring my candle and I will walk around all the mounds of it and I'll ask for the intercession for all the generations for thousands of years, that have gone before me, in *Tlachtga*. And I always ask that it [*Tlachtga*] might be preserved and looked after and minded. And then I'll sit, I'll sit on the ground if it's a dry day on *Tlachtga*, if it's a wet day just put something underneath you, and just sit there and contemplate. Really, it's a magical place and you can feel it, you can feel it in your bones, you really can.

She also related a number of scary stories, one of which was from a neighbour of her parents who has since passed on:

> The old people used to say that there used to be stirrings, and that there used to be things happening around Halloween. They used to say that there was definitely a vibe of a kind of an otherworld on the hill, in their day. And I'm going back, I suppose, the old man I'm talking about now would be over a 100 now. And, he used to say definitely, that you would not go up on the hill, you would not go near it on Halloween night, he said. That was the night for them. It belonged to the world of the spirits, that's what the old people said, it belongs to the spirits and leave them be.

Máiréad remembered various stories from her surrounding neighbours and family friends, from when she was a little girl and up to her adult years. She detailed how the locals always knew there was something otherworldly about the hill and how locals would keep away from the hill on *Samhain* night (November Eve), known today as All Hallows' Eve or Halloween night (*Oíche Shamhna*).

> Now there was a man in there, they used to call him Mickeen Fox. Do you know Johnny Fox? No? Just a little stone cottage at the bottom of the hill? Well, there was an old man in there, and he used to visit our home, I don't know why, but he used to like my mom and dad and he used to come out and visit when we bought the place. And he used to say, that never would anyone from this locality, never go near the hill on Halloween night, he never called

it Halloween night, he called it All Souls' Night. And he said, that never. And my mom used to ask him why? And he would say, 'It would make the hair on your head stand up, Mrs Joyce,' he said.

A ghostly story relates to the postman's brother:

He used to walk out from Athboy, before the post office opened at nine, and he used to walk out from Athboy, at about half six in the morning or seven, and he'd walk up and he'd walk round. And one day, right up on the top of the hill, he saw a little girl, sitting down with a posy of flowers, and she looked at him straight in the eye. And something told him, no this wasn't right, so, he walked down the back roads, went into Athboy and he told his wife. And she said, 'Well let's get into the car and we'll go up.' And this is about twenty/twenty-five years ago, and he came up and there was absolutely not a sign. But until the day he died, he maintained he saw her.

Another story relates to a man from Kildalky (a few miles south of Athboy):

But now, I'll tell you a little story. These are just snip bits of just local folklore. About ten or fifteen years ago, there was a guy ploughing for records (potatoes), now in the same field I told you where the big mounds where. And he was just ploughing, he knew nothing, he's from Kildalky. And um, in a big, big tractor with the lights on, they plough all night here you know, when the weather is good. And, he saw something at … around the graveyard, and he said he (a dark figure) was dressed in this old long garb, and it was in the middle of the night. And, he ploughed down and he came back again, and he said he was still there. And, he said he couldn't make out, it was like he was hovering above the ground … and he just went straight up to the top of the hill and called the lads, 'Come and collect me quickly, I want to get out of this field.' And, he wouldn't plough there ever again at night.

Stories collected by school children during the 1930s as part of the Schools' Folklore Scheme, held in the *Duchas* Schools' Collection, are another rich source of local tradition:

There was a family living in the castle in Rathmore called the Plunkets; Cromwell sent for them and they came on horseback and when Cromwell saw them coming across the fields he fired his cannon and killed them. There were eleven sons and one daughter and their mother. When she saw them being killed she fell down from one of the top stairs and died from the effects of it. Her daughter went to England in a coffin with air holes in it and the ruins of the castle are to be seen yet. There are the ruins of a castle to be seen on the Hill of Ward where *Fionn* and the *Fianna* used to stop for half a year because it was a good place for hunting in olden times. There was a battle fought in the field beside the Hill of Ward.

Collected by F. Sherlock, Rathcarran, Co. Meath

There lived in the Hill Of Ward Wind Mill a little man known as a Leipreachan. He was about a foot high. He was dressed up with a coloured jacket and a peaky cap. Once upon a time James Farrelly of the Hill Of Ward was walking round the Wind Mill he caught the Leipreachan by the neck to see what sort of a man was

The site of Tlachtga as it might have looked in the pre-Christian era.

he, and he said spare me my life and I will show you where there is gold. Mr Farrelly got a sally rod and put it where he said and then he let him go. Then he went home for a spade.

Collected by T. Cassidy, Athboy, Co. Meath

About 260 years ago the people of a certain house in Balrath on awakening one morning found a large stone outside the door. There was the track of a hand on the stone, it was supposed to be thrown from the Hill of Ward.

Collected by Neansai Ní Ghallocbhair, Cloran
and Corcullentry, Co. Westmeath

In those lonely places where there was often found a round ring of green grass, greener than the rest of the grass, was called 'The Fairies Ring'. Fairy people are supposed to live in another vault which runs to the 'Hill of Ward' near Athboy. Music was heard very late at night there.

Collected by Maureen Byre, Batterstown, Co. Meath

There is a fairy fort in the middle of the Fair Green. There is a fence of trees round it.

It is round and there is no hole in the centre of it. There is a fairy fort in Alley's field in the Hill of Ward. There is a tree growing in the middle of a wall. There is also another fairy fort in Kathleens Hill there is a hill and a lot of trees growing round it. It is in Gilstown. There is cave that goes under the town from Bun Boggan to Danes Court. Long ago the people used to hide in it when the Danes were persecuting the Catholics. It is not known who built them. There were fairy people supposed to live in them long ago. The forts are on grazing land no one ever touched them. There was music and dancing heard in Kathleens Hills in Gilstown and there was also light seen at it.

Collected by Mamie Rispin, Athboy Co. Meath

A secret passage was thought by some to run beneath *Tlachtga* to Rathmore Castle. It was also rumoured that there was buried treasure at *Tlachtga* and there are many stories in relation to this. Here is one of them:

Situated near Athboy is the hill of Ward and inside this hill are fairy men guarding a crock of gold. At one time a man by the name of Mr Collins, Freffans, Trim, dug for the gold and as he was digging a little fairy caught hold of him and asked him what was he looking for.

The man said that if the fairy would not get him the pot of gold he would drown him.

As the fairy was getting afraid he leaped from the man's arms. The man kept on but did not find the gold. Again the fairy man appeared and told him to go home and bring back a small bucket and he told him also that he would leave a mark where the gold was then he told him also that the mark was to be a privet stick. The fairy man stuck down the privet and as well as sticking down one he stuck down a great number so that he covered the moat with sticks. When the man who was digging for the gold came back he found to his surprise that the hill was covered with privet sticks so that he did not know which one to dig under.

Collected by John Kelly, Kidalkey, Co. Meath

What is presented here is merely scratching the surface, with its rich history stretching back from Cromwellian times, to the Normans, the turn of the second millennium, the arrival of St Patrick and the legends of the traditions of pagan times going back to 1000 BCE and beyond, there is ample material for imaginative minds to find no end of mythological and spooky stories. *Tlachtga* is without a doubt a treasure trove of inspiration for the traditions and stories that spread to the new world.

CHAPTER 5

The Evolution into Halloween

So, in the preceding chapters we have seen where the traditions of Halloween come from, but that still does not answer the question – how did they come to be distributed so widely across the world? The answer to that question lies in the recolonisation of Ireland in the mid-sixteenth century onwards.

HALLOWEEN – AN IRISH AND BRITISH CULTURAL EXPORT

Following the decision of Henry VIII of England to break with the Roman Catholic Church in 1532, he eventually turned his attention to Ireland during his Dissolution of the Monasteries, which he had undertaken in England first from 1536 onwards. In 1541 the Irish Parliament in Dublin promoted Henry VIII from Lord of Ireland to King of Ireland, giving him authority to further continue the suppression of Catholicism. In reality, the English, at this time, had little control outside the area described as 'The Pale', which was barely 10 per cent of the country. However, during the reign of his daughter, Elizabeth I, the situation changed dramatically and in a very negative way for the native Irish.

A series of punitive wars against the Irish sub-kingdoms led to the beginnings of emigration from Ireland. After the failure of the Irish to win the Nine Years' War at the Battle of Kinsale in 1601, the mass exodus began, compounded by the Flight of the Earls, when Ireland's last hope – Hugh O'Neil and Rory O'Donnell with a large entourage – left Ireland for continental Europe in 1607. The war had almost bankrupted the English government, which led to a terrible retribution – Ireland was raped financially and its subjects were largely reduced to the status of chattels. This led to a wave of emigration that continued (to varying degrees) into the twentieth century.

Those who could afford passage to the New World of the Caribbean or New England bought places upon ships heading west across the Atlantic Ocean. Those who could not afford the fare were forced to go as indentured servants, as a means of paying for their passage. It is a common belief that Irish people were slaves in the New World but this is untrue. The new arrivals from Ireland (short of the fare) were obliged to work for one to four years to pay for their passage by ship. Like the Africans, who arrived as slaves, they spoke no English and were obliged to work on plantations in horrible conditions. The difference was that, after paying off their debt in the plantations of Jamaica, Virginia, or wherever they had ended up, they were free to leave, unlike the African prisoners, who were usually slaves for life.

At the other end of the globe, in Australia and New Zealand, the Irish were arriving in large numbers, but not as indentured servants. Mostly the Irish, Scottish and also many English arriving there were 'criminals', some of whom who had been deported for pathetically minor crimes such as stealing bread to avoid starvation.

In both the Americas and Australasia, the Irish adapted quickly, learned to speak English and often went on to become very successful.

However, they did not forget their own culture, even if they did not retain their language, and it is because of the retention of these hard-to-suppress cultural habits that we find the traditions of Ireland continuing in North America, Australia and New Zealand. But before we look at the somewhat mutated re-export of Irish and Scottish traditions back to Europe, let us take a look at what other people brought with them.

AFRICAN AND CENTRAL/SOUTH AMERICAN TRADITIONS

In North America and the Caribbean (Haiti in particular) we can detect a synthesis of African themes that arrived from the *Vodun* native religion (becoming voodoo), which originated in west and central Africa. It is from these practices that we derive the zombie (*zonbi*), strange objects called 'fetishes', such as statues or dried animal or human parts (a hand, for instance) and also the voodoo doll. These items and the zombie are popular within current Halloween celebrations but have merged via African slaves with the European traditions of the colonists and later arrivals.

In South and Central America and Cuba, aspects of the native religions and *Vodun* have also merged with Roman Catholicism in what is known as *Santería*, which also had an influence on modern Halloween. In Mexico, the Day of the Dead (*Día de los Muertos*) is still celebrated. The origins of the modern Mexican holiday lie in indigenous observances dating back hundreds of years and to an Aztec festival dedicated to the goddess *Mictecacihuatl*. She is literally 'Lady of the Dead' and is queen of *Mictlān*, the Aztec underworld, ruling over the afterlife along with her husband *Mictlāntēcutli*. Her role is to watch over the bones of the dead and preside over the ancient festival of the dead.

Prior to the Spanish colonisation, in the sixteenth century CE, the celebration took place at the beginning of summer. Gradually, it became associated with 31 October to 2 November, to coincide with the western Catholic three days of Halloween (All Saints' Eve), All Saints' Day and All Souls' Day. In the last three decades, particularly since the internet, the Mexican Day of the Dead has become more popular as part of Halloween across the world.

The painted skull is very much a Mexican tradition that we see becoming more popular at Halloween, which interestingly ties in nicely with the Irish cult of the severed head (where the soul resides) that is evident in the second and first millennia BCE. Human sacrifice had once been practised in ancient Celtic Europe and still took place in Mexico at the time of the demise of the Aztecs at the hands of the Spanish invaders in 1521. The heart and innards were offered to the gods and some choice flesh parts were eaten (cannibalism) but other body parts would then be disposed of, the viscera fed to animals, and the severed head placed on display in the *tzompantli* or skull rack. In the modern celebrations the skull is still an important symbol.

IRISH AND BRITISH *SAMHAIN* TRADITIONS

Although a vast number of Halloween/*Samhain* traditions come from Ireland, many of them also come from Britain – Scotland, Wales, Cornwall and parts of England. Similar traditions have also survived to some extent in continental Europe, particularly Brittany. The traditions in Ireland have been covered to some degree in relation to *Tlachtga*, but let us now take a wider look at the *Samhain* traditions.

On the Isle of Man, New Year's Day was regarded as 1 November until relatively recently. The mummers play, a form of re-enactment of old pagan beliefs, would take place with mummers going from door to door on Halloween, singing a song, 'Tonight is New Year's Night, Hop-tu-Naa!' Children also participated by going around begging and saying rhymes or giving some other kind of performance. This echoes down to the modern day with 'trick or treat' often involving a song, dance or some kind of performance on the doorstep in return for some 'treat', usually sweets or cake. In Britain, particularly England and Northern Ireland, the tradition is displaced to 5 November with children begging 'a penny for the Guy', which is a stuffed effigy of Guido (Guy) Fawkes to be burned on the bonfire, although in Northern Ireland this was/is sometimes an effigy of the Catholic Pope.

Also popular throughout the British Isles was for young people to get up to harmless mischief – for instance removing doors from sheds, moving items to unusual places and letting cows out of a field, etc. It was common for young people to impersonate the spirits of the land, but now the American custom of dressing up in scary costumes has become popular.

Joe McGowan recounts in *Echoes of a Savage Land* how it used to be growing up in Sligo (north-west Ireland):

Years ago there were no trick-or-treaters in Sligo. But the spirits were out! Evidence of the previous night's activities greeted churchgoers as they walked to mass on All Saint's Day; carts left with one wheel or no wheels, gates missing, cabbage-strewn roads … A favourite trick was to fasten the front and back door of a neighbour's house from the outside and then climb up on the roof and block the chimney, sending clouds of smoke into the kitchen below.

Another choice prank was to take the cart up to a gate, bringing the shafts through the bars and then harness the ass to the other side. This was quite an unusual sight in the morning and very funny, to everyone except the owner of the team.

… a farmer well known for his bad humour kept the whole parish amused for days with his efforts to chase away a 'strange' horse, which was later revealed, after a shower of rain, to be his own horse, disguised by a coat of whitewash.

In modern Ireland such pranks are still fairly popular – such as turning road signs to point the wrong way or leaving traffic cones in silly places. More common generally across Ireland and in most countries is the 'trick-or-treat', which more often than not involves a treat. However, some tricks do happen – like blue mouth or pepper sweets and being sprayed with water pistols and being targeted by firecrackers or buckets of water, etc.

In Ireland the *Tuatha Dé Danann* were considered to have power over the fertility of the land, and similar beliefs existed in parts of Britain. It was thought necessary to placate them as they could bring either prosperity or plague and famine – sick cattle and poor harvests. People acknowledged this power and made offerings on the ground, usually of milk, sometimes meat (pork most often) and also cakes. This would occur at the four Celtic feasts, including *Samhain*.

It was also common at *Samhain* for people in masks (mummers) and suits, traditionally of straw, to go around villages and towns to beg for food, drink or money. If people were stingy they were thought to receive bad luck and misfortune in the year ahead. In some cases, this tradition has trans-ferred from the Celtic New Year to the modern New Year. In Scotland, the Hogmanay tradition was of a fire in the kitchen centre that the mummers/guisers would dance around clockwise/sunwise (*iompú deiseal*) if they were well looked after. This was thought to bring the household good luck, but if they danced *tuathal* or anticlockwise then this would bring the opposite – bad luck on the household who had been ungenerous! The following rhyme was sung to encourage the household to be generous:

Hogmanay, trololay give us your white bread and none of your grey. Get up and gie's our Hogmanay!

A similar tradition survives today in Dingle, Ireland, on St Stephen's Day/Wren Day (26 December), perhaps again transferred from *Samhain*. Teams of people (including musicians) representing different streets or areas of the town (mostly men) go around the whole town in straw costumes and get progressively more drunk. When teams encounter one another they have a mock battle. After it is over, those not fit only for bed retire to the pub and more drink is taken.

In some cases the *Samhain* or Christmas/New Year processions involve a horse character, often with snapping jaws, called the white mare, hobby horse, *Láir Bhán* (Irish) or *Mari Lwyd* (Welsh), representing the *sidhe* (*Tuatha Dé Danann*) spirits of the land riding forth across the land. In Limerick it was called the 'Blanket Horse' (*Capall an tSusa*) and across the country the horse's entourage were called names such as strawboys (*buachaillí tuí*), guisers, hugadais or visards. To show disrespect to the *Lár/Láir Bhán* and its entourage was to invite famine, disaster and general bad luck on yourself and your household.

Some believed that at *Samhain* the fairies could turn the yellow-flowered weed, ragwort (gone to seed usually), called *buachalán buí*, into spirit horses and use them to ride about all night long. Sometimes a human might be able to join them, so long as they did as they were told. In one story, a young fellow is invited by the king of the fairies to ride with them on a white calf but told not to speak. In their adventures they ride over to Scotland but after the young man lets out an exclamation about the calf making an excellent jump the fairies all disappear, leaving him a journey of more than a day to get back home to Ireland.

It was considered advisable to stay well clear of graveyards on Halloween night as the dead might well rise. Some considered that to see a ghost or risen dead person at *Samhain* would cause instant death!

Staying clear of ringforts, barrows and burial mounds was also considered to be a wise move, as it was often believed that lights and sounds of dancing and laughter could be heard at *Samhain* as the *sidhe* came out into the world. It was also thought that the spirits of the dead could emerge into the world of the living through these places. Equally, the *sidhe* or the dead might kidnap the living, bring them gallivanting or even back to the otherworld:

> It is considered on All Hallows' Eve, hob-goblins, evil spirits and fairies hold high revel and that they are traveling abroad in great numbers. The dark and sullen Phooka (*púca*) is then particularly mischievous and many mortals are abducted to fairyland. Those persons taken away to the raths are often seen at this time by their living friends, and usually accompanying a fairly cavalcade. If you meet the fairies, it is said, on All Hallows' Eve, and throw the dust taken from under your feet at them, they will be obliged to surrender any captive human being belonging to their company.
>
> Lageniensis, *Irish Folklore*, 1870

In conversation with Breton Druidess Rachel Scoazec and her mother Micheline (aged 93 at time of publication), they described to me the Halloween traditions that had survived in Brittany. Rachel explained to me the context of these traditions was a background of suppression of the Breton culture beginning around 1940 and continuing to the 1970s. Around the mid-1970s the Breton language was more accepted and there was the beginnings of a bilingual revival in Brittany. Prior to this, all aspects of the culture and folklore were discouraged by the French government. Bretons were made to feel ashamed of their own cultural heritage, encouraged to accept the modern French way of life and stop speaking their own language. From Rachel's and Micheline's descriptions, the Breton customs bore many similarities to those of Britain and Ireland:

> It was not a French thing and Brittany is not like France. There was no tradition of Halloween as such in France, the Gaulish culture had been completely eradicated long ago. Western Brittany became Frenchified about 300 years after the eastern side. On that night most of France would have done nothing at all, only celebrate All Saints' Day, in the Catholic tradition. In Brittany it was a different thing, some Bretons did not want anything to do with the old traditions, being very Catholic, but the others did. Different old Breton traditions existed depending on whether you lived on the coast or inland, my family come from the west coast and kept up the old traditions.

They went on to describe what they actually did on *Samhain* night:

> The customs survived because of the strong spirit of death in all these Breton traditions, it's called *Ankou*, and it's even a taboo word. *Ankou* would be death itself. A Breton term *Kalan Goañv* would be the calends of winter, a transitional period between the clear season and the dark season, and for agricultural people like the Bretons it was a time when crops would be collected, wood stacked and livestock put in the sheds. So then, if you lived inland, or by the coast it would be different. Inland, people would be careful about going out on the 31st of October. They would

try not to go out because they might meet '*Lavandiere De La Nuit*', the washerwoman washing your shroud – a figure of death, another figure would be 'the black dog' or '*l'Ankou*', a ghostly figure with a scythe.

Another connection with death would be horses. You could be in the countryside and if you left your horses out overnight [on 31 October] death can travel via the horse. If you leave the horses out during that particular night, when the veils are thin between the two worlds – the world of the living and the world of the dead, the horse can carry death on its back, and helps death do its business quicker. The next morning, the farmers on the 1st of November, if they saw their horses very sweaty and tired, would not give them any work and leave them rest and give them feed, as they knew that they had been used by death during the night.

A similar tradition to the mummers of Ireland, in particular, also existed:

There is such a huge culture of death in Brittany. People talk about the dead all the time in Brittany, it's very morbid, but it can either be scary or joyous or very sad. There is tradition of old men and old women singers in Brittany coming from door to door in the night and keen for your dead. You're supposed to give them money, and if you don't there will be problems for you throughout the year. They're not just singing, they are channelling the dead and their requests, because the dead come at that time … If you listen to the voice, it's like a sepulchral voice … it's in the tome of the voice, they have a particular sound that is in the tradition, it's like an otherworldy sound, like channelling the Cailleach in Ireland.

In the house you light a big fire and remove the tripod for the cooking cauldron. You would put fresh white linen on the table with a bowl of *lait ribot* (buttermilk) and pancakes for the dead. It would be left for the souls of the dead – the *Anaon*. So basically you are preparing a good fire and a good table with food on out of respect to welcome the souls of the dead so they can have a bit of heat, as it's cold outside.

My grandmother would tell me to walk in the middle of the road, outside on that night because on the sides of roads the gorse of furze thorns would be full of the souls of the dead. Up to 700 souls would be in gathered in each thorn and you would avoid disturbing them by staying in the middle.

Apples were an important part of the night:

Another thing was to put candles by the wind and to eat apples and hazelnuts, especially apples (*aval*) because of the magical connection with Avalon, Breton culture is related to the Welsh and Cornish traditions. For instance, you would play divination games with the apple pips – you would take two pips put onto a hot poker near the fire and from the reaction of the pips you would see if you were going to be lucky in love or stay with your beloved.

If you can peel an apple without breaking the skin and throw it over your shoulder – how it falls gives you a letter and that would be the initial of your lover.

Some traditions were particular to the coastline:

If you lived by the coast, (Brittany has a coastline of over 1,000km), so the souls of the dead, of those who drowned in the sea, would be seen and heard, and the men called it *Yann an Aod*. Basically you would not go out at night because you would hear all the dead of the sea. With the ocean there's a lot of fear, there's a place in the very west of Brittany, near Audierne is called *Baie des Trepassés* (the Bay of The Dead) and at that time of year they come back on the wind and they scream and you can hear their haunting voices on the wind and it's very scary.

You do still have a lot of the fear in the people, for example on the islands. I remember one time someone opened the door and saying to me, 'Oh I was frightened, I saw your face and you were coming from the island to tell me someone has died.' Because the island around the west coast of Brittany called *Enez Sun* had women there like Druidesses. Still nowadays they would be involved with being a death *dula* or death Shaman. They would pass souls to the otherside, plus they would also come to you. Also there was the great fear with some traditions like *Lavandiere de la Mort*. You try not to go out, but if you saw the washerwoman during the night washing a death shroud it meant it's for you. And usually during that night, if you see her in the window you may get the names of the people who are going to die during the year, but you would not really want that.

One scary story she described was:

There is a story I remember of a young woman who was too poor to buy her wedding dress and she got cursed by the bride-groom's side who did not want the marriage. They were more well-to-do and didn't want her associated with them. This girl, it would have been about 1914 or 1915, and she went to the graveyard to ask the dead ancestors for pearls to pay for the wedding dress, and she said she got them.

She explained a little about superstitious practices:

> There was a lot of *intersignes*, it has always been the case. There is a superstitious mindset of people, who would read something from the behaviour of a crow or other natural signs or you do things or not do things: you would not eat the food for the dead on the table, you would remove the tripod from the fire so the dead don't burn themselves on it, you walk in the middle of the road so not to crush the dead souls. You would perhaps go to the cemetery to speak to your dead ancestors. You never talk about the *Ankou* in Brittany, people look at you funny. There's a lot of taboos around death, especially at this time of year. People are not supposed to have anything done late because it could be a problem for next year – you have your wood stacked and all the harvest done by this time.

As mentioned earlier, the bonfire was a big tradition at *Samhain*, throughout the British Isles. While this still remains a big tradition in Britain, along with fireworks (5 November), it is less common in Ireland now at Halloween, but fireworks are still popular at this time. In the past people would light the fire and pray for the dead, kneeling down in front of it. Also common to England and Ireland, farmers and country people would traverse their fields, in a sunwise direction, with flaming torches or bunches of blazing straw to bless the land and protect it from malign influences (witches in particular).

In Scotland it was common to light a fire on top of a barrow, tumulus or burial mound. An example in Perthshire was the building of a fire by everyone of the community on a 'Mound of the Dead', which was then lit by an old man or several older men. Everyone would dance around the fire and pass around the local area with brands or torches lit from the fire.

In Britain and Ireland new fire was brought into the house from the bonfire to light the hearth fires that had been put out before nightfall. This on a smaller scale echoes the lighting of the royal fire at Tara (probably from the *Tlachtga* fire) and the subsequent lighting of fires across the country. This tradition has been transferred to Christmas in many cases with the lighting of the Yule log.

In Wales people jumped through the fire and when it had gone out rushed away to escape from the 'black sow', who was thought to take hold of the slowest person. This act was supposed to bring good luck and health and may be linked with the sun's power symbolised by the fire. A similar tradition of fire jumping exists at the direct opposite time of the year, *Bealtaine*.

In Ireland, fires are far less common than a few decades ago, but in Dublin in particular, the Halloween bonfire tradition still survives, although it is discouraged by police for health and safety reasons.

HALLOWEEN FOOD

Food played a very important role in Halloween, especially in Ireland, and this has been explored in some detail by Regina Sexton of University College, Cork. She writes that much of our knowledge of nineteenth- and twentieth-century Irish Halloween customs, particularly surrounding food, comes from the Schools' Collection of the National Folklore Collection. From my own investigations of the same source material, I can confirm that it is indeed a rich source of material, collected by children in the 1930s. It details many culinary traditions that are no longer with us and also those that had already died out or become scarce by the time the details were committed to writing.

Food activities took place before the evening meal, the Halloween meal itself and post-meal festivities. Pre-meal snacks might include apples or toffee apples and nuts, or even a boxty (potato pancakes). The Halloween meal itself would generally include a savoury and sweet bread/cake, with potatoes (obviously from the 1600s onwards) usually being a major component. Colcannon (mashed potato with cabbage or kale) was very popular but also various forms of boxty was common. In addition, cabbage, kale, onion, turnips, beans, hazelnuts, herring, sloes, apples and peas might also feature in the meal or in the divination games and activities afterwards. The use or absence of salt was also of some significance. A bread of cakes was also eaten at the meal, either a home-made or shop-bought barmbrac, oaten cakes (especially in Northern counties) or even a sweet variant of boxty. In more affluent times, in the twentieth century, urban celebrations of more affluent families did include more exotic ingredients such as oranges, grapes and coconuts.

More detail on traditional Halloween food was collected by author Florence Irwin between 1905 and 1919 for her 1949 book *The Cookin' Woman: Irish Country Recipes & Others*. One excerpt, on Halloween, shows that traditions varied considerably across the country:

No other day is Ireland is celebrated by so many special dishes. They are all vegetarian, of course but are so popular that they provide real feasts on Halloweve night. County Armagh celebrates with potato apple dumpling, and potato apple cake. Counties Tyrone, Cavan, Fermanagh and Londonderry indulge in boxty pancakes, boxty dumplings, boxty bread, potato pudding and colcannon. No matter which is the dish chosen for Halloweve night's fast (or feast), a wedding ring carefully wrapped in grease-proof paper … is put into it.

Some of these culinary traditions have survived up until today, some have not. Perhaps the most common survival is the barmbrac, although today it usually a worthless ring, baked into the loaf but not wrapped in greaseproof paper, as in earlier times. Many of these old traditions are associated with special activities such as food for the fairies (*sidhe*) and the dead, or as part of Halloween games, usually connected with divination in some form.

Food was also left for the fairies specifically, to appease them on Halloween night. A portion of mashed potato or colcannon might be left by the hearth or possibly outside the house. Oatcakes were often left for the fairies in Donegal, milk was a popular offering to the fairies and regional variations applied, as with the Halloween food in general. The Schools Collection provides another interesting account, from Co. Galway, in relation to the fairies:

The first plate of this colcannon is kept for the fairies lest they should be hungry while changing from the Summer residence to their Winter home. No salt should be put on their portion.

REMEMBERING THE DEAD

In ancient times sacrifices were offered to the spirits of the dead but over time this evolved. It was a common tradition in Ireland, Scotland and Brittany to leave food out for the dead on *Samhain*. In some cases it was sufficient just to set a place at the table for the dead. The tradition of leaving food for the dead has mutated somewhat, with people eating special Halloween food – the barmbrac (barmbrack) in Scotland and Ireland, which often contains a ring, considered lucky for the finder. In Wales and Brittany it was common on All Souls' Eve for groups of people to go from house to house asking for 'soul cakes' in exchange for promising to pray for the ancestors of that household. Various treats were consumed at *Samhain* despite the relative lack of abundance. Today fancy foods, chocolate, sugar and confectionary are widely available and cheap – this was not the case even fifty years ago. The practice of leaving actual food out for the dead is no longer common, even though food is far cheaper and more abundant than it has ever been in the past.

It has been suggested that the giving of food echoes the sacrifices of an earlier time. Geoffrey Keating speculated that sacrifices of animals, or even humans, were made at *Samhain* into the bonfire, not for the dead but to placate vegetal spirits and ensure good harvests for the coming year. Sometimes this spirit was symbolised by a sheaf of corn, with some of these traditions being transferred to Christmas rather than Halloween. In accounts of the ancient Gauls and the Irish it is suggested that orgiastic rites took place and human sacrifices. Offerings of humans to the Fomorians and to *Crom Curaich/Cruach* at *Samhain* were thought to placate the forces of blight and destruction and keep disaster at bay. Whether these stories are genuine or just Christian propaganda remains to be proven. However, memory of such stories survives in stories of witches, ghouls, ghosts and zombies who might take our lives or even our souls at Halloween.

A common theme of the past was the lighting of candles for the ancestors as a mark of respect and also as an invitation for them to return to the family homestead. In the past, poorer people would make a lantern by carving out a turnip to house the light. This tradition was exported to America and Canada and mutated slightly to become pumpkin lanterns, as these are both larger and much easier to cut open and hollow out. Of course, this is the source of the current tradition that has been imported to Europe and many places around the world that otherwise would have no interest in or knowledge of pumpkins. In many cases, pumpkins are

Turnip lanterns – the precursor of the pumpkin lantern commonly made today.

not eaten in Europe and beyond and are only bought because of their Halloween associations.

On All Souls' Day, which is 2 November, Christian tradition is to remember the dead, with masses being said for the dead, and it is also a popular day to visit or tidy up the graves of the deceased. This is clearly a Christian replacement for the earlier pagan tradition, but the folk beliefs of the return of the dead continued into the twentieth century and are still held by some today.

GAMES

At the *aonach* (assembly) both secular and religious activities took place and these generally included games, races and dancing – perhaps the most famous being the *Lughnasadh* assembly at Teltown (*Tailteann*) in August, which was well known for horse racing. Horse racing is still part of August celebrations – a modern hangover from this tradition is the Dingle Races, which opens for three days only, Friday to Sunday, in the second week of August.

Similar in essence to this survival are the games played at Halloween, derived from a much older tradition. Up until the second half of the twentieth century it was popular to play apple bobbing games – ducking the head into a barrel or a large bowl to retrieve them. Another game was to tie an apple hanging from the ceiling or cross-beam with a string – the purpose was to try and take a bite without using your hands, which is much harder than it sounds. A more dangerous version involved a stick hung horizontally, with an apple on one end and a candle at the other – again the purpose was to try and take a bite of apple, but without getting scorched. A more modern version of this game substituted a potato for the candle as a safer alternative, and in Scotland a bannock covered with treacle or honey is used. In this modern version, the person is blindfolded and cannot see which they are eating. Another variant on the apple bobbing was ducking your head into a basin to try and collect (with your mouth) the coins left in the bottom. When I was a child, toffee apples (on a stick and covered with red toffee) were still common Halloween fare, a treat that was not available during other times of the year. Of course, apples are not only plentiful at this time of year but they are also strongly connected with the otherworld, as discussed earlier.

Another popular game was a bit like 'chicken' – young people, men or boys especially, spent the night at a haunted location or visited a graveyard at midnight to test their bravery (or stupidity, some might say). Some people still do this even today.

DIVINATION

Halloween was considered an auspicious time to try to predict the future, despite specific instructions by the Catholic Church not to do so, these activities persisted into the modern era, not just in Ireland but throughout Celtic countries.

Going back into pre-Christian Ireland, *Daithi* (fifth-century CE High King of Ireland) is reputed to have been at *Cnoc an Draoi* (Hill of the Druids) in Sligo at Halloween. He is said to have ordered his chief Druid to forecast the future for the whole year ahead, until next *Samhain*. The Druid spent the night on the hill top and on the following morning revealed his predictions, which were said to have come true.

Over time, this evolved into simple divination techniques or games. Nut shells were burned in the fire and the ashes were used to predict the future. The person finding a ring in the *báirín breac* (barmbrac) was thought to be the next person in the house to get married. In Sligo a more complex tradition existed with a ring, a nut, a button and a penny being cooked in the barmbrac. The finder of the nut would never marry, the finder of the ring would marry soon, the finder of the button would become a tailor and the finder of the penny would become rich! Similar traditions existed elsewhere in Ireland with different items – wood chip (beaten by spouse), rag (poverty), pea and bean (wealth), religious medal (joining priesthood or order).

A popular activity, particularly among young women, was divination to ascertain what kind of marriage partner they would have in the future, which was popular throughout the British Isles. Different techniques were used, depending on the region, but hazelnuts seem to have been a popular method. Two nuts (given names) were placed on glowing embers and if they jumped towards each other then matrimony was likely. The faster this happened, the more certain it was.

Another technique was to borrow an apple and place it under the pillow, cut in two, and then go to sleep. It was said that the future husband would be revealed in a dream. In Ireland, Brittany and Scotland a whole apple peel, thrown over the left shoulder at midnight, was then put on the ground and the initial of the future husband would hopefully be seen in the shape of the peel.

Various other marriage divination methods involved a head of cabbage, molten lead, eating three salted herring, horse shoe nails, yarrow plants and raking hay at midnight. A bizarre method used by young ladies was to visit a lime kiln (no longer in existence) and throw a ball of wool into the kiln while holding the end. Retrieving the ball by winding it in might reveal the name of a future husband.

GHOSTS, BANSHEES, DEVILS AND WEREWOLVES

Divination was popular but also considered dangerous – deals with the Devil to know the future could be disastrous. Halloween was, and still is, a time when many people like to give themselves a good scare and test their bravery. To this day, it is popular for young people and ghost hunters to visit supposedly haunted places, particularly around Halloween.

Britain and Ireland are full of stories around 'the quare fellow', 'old Nick', 'Satan', etc., many of them associated with Halloween. One particular story, regarding Loftus Hall (formerly Redmond Hall), in Co. Wexford that I have visited, describes how the Devil jumped through the ceiling and roof in 1775, leaving a hole that was there for well over a hundred years. Following its restoration, the house is open to tourists and is still regarded as one of the most haunted places in Ireland.

Ireland and Scotland are two places that are full of folklore with regard to werewolves, and the medical condition of lycanthropy is thought to be the source of these legends. There are many stories of people, and even entire households, transforming into wolves (not wolf-like creatures), not necessarily at the full moon. It is known that ancient clans often had totem animals associated with them, such as the wolf; perhaps these stories are somehow associated with totemic animals.

Historically, werewolves are also strongly linked with Greek and Norse legends. With the huge influx of Vikings into both Britain and Ireland it is quite possible that Norse legends influenced British and Irish werewolf traditions. In the Middle Ages, werewolves were thought mostly to be created by witches, and the two became closely associated. Just as thousands of accused witches were put to death, thousands of accused werewolves were similarly dispatched, most often on flimsy evidence.

The modern stories of werewolves are very much derived from the eighteenth century onwards, with Hollywood films popularising the wolfman type, generally transforming at the full moon and needing a silver bullet to kill them.

The banshee (*Bean Sí*) is a female spirit who appears to herald the death of a person. Written accounts of this rather morbid fairy woman go back to the fourteenth century in both Gaelic and Norman accounts. By tradition, they appear to a member or members of a family when one of the family is about to die. In some cases there is a knocking heard or a terrible wail or scream from the banshee, reminiscent of the 'keening' wail of mourning women (*bean chaointe*). The appearance of the banshee can vary greatly, but regardless of looks is said to appear to one or more family members when a death is due, whatever their location in the world. A banshee can be attached to certain families down the generations, usually of Gaelic Irish heritage, and I have personal experience of such people who claim to have heard the banshee themselves, or of the banshee being present throughout their family history.

WITCHES

Witches have been very much associated with Halloween since the demise of paganism throughout Europe at various times. Christianity took hold in Britain early but faded with Saxon invasions, re-established largely with the help of Irish missionaries from the sixth century onwards. Scandinavia was late in becoming Christianised, which took place well into the tenth century when they capitulated to external pressures to convert. Clearly, from the establishment of Christianity the previous pagan religions were demonised, with Druids, pagan priests, etc. characterised as evil witches, warlocks, wizards, necromancers and even Devil worshippers. Even faith healers, fairy doctors and wise women/men (*bean feasa/banfhaidh*) – in fact, anyone linked with the old pre-Christian culture and knowledge, could be labelled as a witch.

In the New World, bringing your old culture with you was not looked upon so negatively, except in Puritan areas (e.g. Salem, which is famous for its witch trials). The notion of witchcraft was not attached to old European traditions with such great fervour as was to be found during the Reformation and Counter Reformation of Europe. The witch is a common feature in fairy stories (e.g. *Hansel and Gretel*) and generally has extremely negative overtones, even modern tales such as those of Hans Christian Andersen (e.g. *The Little Mermaid*, 1837) and L. Frank Baum (e.g. *The Wonderful Wizard of Oz*, 1900) tended to portray them as evil or ambivalent. In Britain, witchcraft was illegal until 1950 and ten years later it was legalised in the USA. It did not, however, become legal in Ireland until the 1980s.

Although modern forms of Druidry/Druidism and also witchcraft (such as Wicca) are now legal, witchcraft is still portrayed in a negative light, especially in modern pop culture surrounding Halloween. In truth, modern witches can be good, bad or ambivalent, just like any spiritual practitioner – the pop-cultural perception is very much a hangover from Christian ideology, that has generally disparaged any form of spirituality that isn't Christian.

VAMPIRES

Vampires are part of world mythology – from vampiric creatures found in the legends of India, Mesopotamia, Rome and Greece. The vampire as we know it originates in eastern and southern Europe, becoming first mentioned in the English language (as vampyre) in 1734, in a travelogue titled *Travels of Three English Gentlemen*. The first work of modern English fiction featuring vampires was John Polidori's the *The Vampyre* published in 1819.

Following this, the genre of horror fiction began to take shape, including the 1818 novel from Polidori's friend, Mary Shelley: *Frankenstein, or The Modern Prometheus*, which was hugely successful shortly after its publication. In Ireland, Joseph Sheridan Le Fanu had a vampire novella *Carmilla* published in 1872, which could possibly have influenced another Irishman, Bram Stoker.

The most famous vampire of all, Dracula, was created by Stoker, from Dublin, in part from legends of Vlad III (the Impaler, of Wallachia). However, it may also have been inspired by the story of *Abhartach/ Avartagh* in Patrick Weston-Joyce's *The Origin and History of Irish Names of Places*, published in 1875. It's interesting to note the belief that evil beings or people had 'bad blood'. In Irish language that translates as '*Droch fhola*', pronounced as droc-ula, which in fact sounds more similar to 'Dracula' than the patronymic title of Vlad III – *Dracul* (meaning dragon).

Stoker's infamous novel *Dracula* was published in 1897, featuring a Transylvanian count, but it is quite possible that he had read Weston-Joyce's book, which was published four years before Stoker and his wife (Florence Balcombe) moved from Dublin to London. Certainly the prospect of him finding inspiration in a recently published Irish vampire story seems too likely to be ignored:

> There is a place in the parish of Errigal in Derry, called Slaghtaverty, but it ought to have been called Laghtaverty, the *laght* or sepulchral monument of the *abhartach* [*avartagh*] or dwarf.

This dwarf was a magician, and a dreadful tyrant, and after having perpetrated great cruelties on the people he was at last vanquished and slain by a neighbouring chieftain; some say by *Fionn Mac Cumhail.* He was buried in a standing posture, but the very next day he appeared in his old haunts, more cruel and vigorous than ever. And the chief slew him a second time and buried him as before, but again he escaped from the grave, and spread terror through the whole country. The chief then consulted a druid, and according to his directions, he slew the dwarf a third time, and buried him in the same place, with his head downwards; which subdued his magical power, so that he never again appeared on earth. The *laght* raised over the dwarf is still there, and you may hear the legend with much detail from the natives of the place, one of whom told it to me.

Weston-Joyce, *The Origin and History of Irish Names of Places*

Both Stoker's *Dracula* and Le Fanu's *Carmilla* have been the basis for a massive number of vampire horror films, beginning with the Hungarian feature film *Drakula halála* (Károly Lajthay, 1921). This continued in 1922 with German director Friedrich Wilhelm Murnau's much more successful *Nosferatu*, which was based on Stoker's *Dracula* and became quite a sensation. One could claim that the vampire is more popular today than it has ever been, having featured in hundreds of books and films, including the popular *Twilight* saga. Although there is little to actually link vampires to Halloween or *Samhain*, it is very much part of the cannon of evil or scary creatures that feature in modern Halloween celebrations.

֍

Over time we can see a transition from pagan practices to survivals into the Christian era. Christianity mutated the traditions of Britain, Ireland and continental Europe, but it is clear that many of the old traditions survived, albeit sometimes stripped of their original meaning. As we moved into the modern age, traditions continued, especially in rural areas, with home-made costumes, home-made foods, home-made decorations and games taking place in the home or in the village/town.

With the invention of the radio, television and the beginnings of cheap international travel (from the 1950s onwards), we can see a clear migration of Halloween traditions from North America back to Europe, from where they originated. Of course, with the mixing of cultures and the passing of time, they have mutated and been transformed to a large extent. This has been further transformed by popular culture, particularly the horror genre in both books and films. However, along with the revival of paganism in Europe and North America (in particular), there has been renewed interest in the customs and practices of the ancient pagans of the pre-Christian era and also pagan survivals that endured into fairly recent times, as we shall see in the next chapter.

People dancing around the bonfire on Samhain night.

CHAPTER 6

The Neo-Pagan Revival of Samhain

Tlachtga Lady Goddess Fair
Come to us on frosted air
Guide our path by pale moonlight
Light our fires on *Samhain* night.

Gavin Bone

The Druid revival can be said to have started in England with antiquary, natural philosopher and writer John Aubrey (1626–97), who had a particular interest in Stonehenge, near Salisbury, England. Irish philosopher and writer John Toland (1670–1722) was inspired by Aubrey's work and wrote a history of the Druids as well as holding the first modern Druid revival meeting in 1717. Toland may well have known William Stukeley (1687–1765), who was an English antiquarian, physician and highly eccentric Anglican clergyman. From this small start, the revival orders of modern Druidry/Druidism were formed in the eighteenth century, gaining popularity in the following centuries. The Celtic Twilight, of the 1800s in Ireland particularly, renewed interest in all things Celtic – the language and culture of Wales, Ireland and Scotland, which has continued to gather pace in the twentieth century onwards.

Witchcraft remained fairly underground in both North America and Europe until the late nineteenth century – with the Golden Dawn in Britain and Ireland being far from secret, which although not described as witchcraft was certainly magical and esoteric. With the legalisation of witchcraft, figures such as Gerald Gardner became prominent (author of *Witchcraft Today* and the founder of the Wicca neo-pagan religion) and many neo-pagan and neo-Druid organisations were founded, particularly from the 1950s onwards. Much of the Druid revival in Britain was linked with the Freemason organisation, but as time has progressed Druidry/Druidism has returned to its Celtic origins, moving further and further away from its Romantic influences. To some extent, the same has happened in witchcraft, with an increase in Celtic influence – although most forms tends to remain largely syncretic and a synthesis of many different pagan formats.

With witchcraft no longer being illegal, although often frowned upon, the ancient pagan festivals (called Sabbats by Wiccans) could be celebrated by all manner of neo-pagans without fear of being arrested. *Samhain*, in both witchcraft and Druid traditions, has been well established as the pagan New Year and, of course, this has led to a revival of this festival in particular.

In my lifetime (since 1970), there has been a massive increase in interest in all things esoteric and in non-conventional spirituality, although this really began a decade earlier with the hippie movement and transfer of esoteric ideas from 'folk tradition' and the exotic 'East' to Europe and America. By the time I was an adult, the neo-pagan movement had become quite well established but, since the creation of the internet, it has mushroomed considerably all around the world. Of course, Ireland, formerly a deeply conservative and mostly Roman Catholic country, has not remained untouched by this and the last three decades have seen a massive increase in both practising neo-pagans and interest in the Celtic past of Ireland.

REVIVAL AT *TLACHTGA*

According to Michelle Alú, author John Gilroy spent four years of research before completing *Tlachtga: Celtic Fire Festival* in 1998, which emphasised the importance of the site to the pre-Christian Irish culture and society. Gilroy noted that the Hill of Tara, the neighbouring site renowned as the seat of the High Kings of Ireland, had unfortunately 'overshadowed' *Tlachtga*. Tara was the most prominent site, certainly with regard to the High King, provincial kings and the ruling class. Tara has remained a popular site, both with tourists and Irish people with an interest in spiritual/religious and historical aspects of Ireland. Thousands of people visit Tara every year, but few people make the trip to the Hill of Ward to visit the *Tlachtga* site. To a large extent, it was Gilroy's book that ignited the resurgence of interest in ancestral and ancient practices at *Tlachtga*, as local Meath resident and pagan priestess Gemma McGowan recalls:

> The resurgence of the festival started in 1999. It was started by a local historian called Joe Conlon, with the Athboy heritage forum. The year before that in 1998, John Gilroy had published a book called *Tlachtga: Celtic Fire Festival*. And that was the thing that really prompted the want to increase attention for that particular hilltop, which had been mostly forgotten in lieu of places like Tara or *Sliabh na Calliagh*. Even though this had been an enormously prominent part of the sacred and political landscape of Meath, it hadn't been in use for nearly a thousand years and had been very much forgotten in terms of the history and the people's attachment to the place. So, there was this want to increase awareness of the hill amongst the Conlon family, the Athboy heritage forum and a number of local people. Thirteen people went up there

in 1999 on Halloween night and lit a fire. They did the same thing a year later in 2000 and in 2001 Joe Conlon approached a number of Druids in the local community and asked them to hold ceremony and the following year that invitation went out to the wider Pagan community.

The first ceremonies, from 31 October 2000 onwards, were organised by Wiccan priestess Janet Farrar and Wiccan priest Gavin Bone. Farrar, together with her now deceased husband Stuart, had introduced Wicca to Ireland after they moved from England in 1976. Eventually settling in Kells, Co. Meath (a fifteen-minute drive from *Tlachtga*), they became leading figures in the Irish esoteric scene, particularly as they both wrote books on the subject. Gavin Bone joined their household in 1996 and co-wrote two books with the Farrars. Following the death of Stuart Farrar in early 2000, Janet Farrar and Gavin Bone continued to live and work together, both as Wiccan practitioners and as authors.

Around 2001 neo-Druid organisation Druidschool began a *Samhain* pilgrimage, focusing on their interpretation of indigenous Druid practices, at *Tlachtga*, Tara and Loughcrew. This did not clash with the locally organised celebrations, as this was not undertaken on 31 October, but on Old Halloween (usually around 5/6 November). I participated in one of these pilgrimages, in 2004, which also involved a visit to *An Tobar Druí* (the Druid's Well) to the south of *Tlachtga* hill. These pilgrimages by Druidschool (now renamed as Celtic Druid Temple) continued for some time, although their current status is unknown to the author.

Subsequent to their initial involvement at *Tlachtga*, Farrar and Bone handed over organising the ceremonies/performance for *Samhain* to priestess Gemma McGowan in 2010. Festivities were based around a pageant/play, re-enacting the *Metrical Dindshenchas* version of the

Straw sun wheel, used at the 2018 Tlachtga fire festival, at the Hill of Ward site.

story of *Tlachtga*, *Mogh Ruith* and Simon Magus, and it also included a contained bonfire. Talking to Michelle Alú in 2019, McGowan stated:

> We tell *Tlachtga's* story on that hill, because it is telling everybody how the hill got its name, it's telling the origin story of that hill. It's also telling the story of again, a very much forgotten sorceress, or possibly a Goddess of the *Fir Bolg*, who died on the hill giving birth to her two sons, casting a huge sovereignty spell with her last dying breath, claiming as long as her three sons' names were remembered, no foe would claim the sovereignty of Ireland. When we go and we tell her story, we are remembering the origins of the hill, we are remembering the name the ancestors gave to the hill, because in recent times it has become known as the hill of Ward. We are remembering the magic associated with the hill. And by calling out the names of her sons, we are calling back the sovereignty for the people of Ireland and for our own personal sovereignty.

Local politicians from Meath County Council, in co-operation with Irish tourist organisation *Fáilte* Ireland, took over the running of the *Samhain* festival of fire in 2018. After marketing consultations it was rebranded as the *Púca* Festival. The festival took place in three locations – Athboy, Drogheda and Trim, with events sponsored by *Fáilte* Ireland. Although the ceremony at *Tlachtga* was not organised directly by *Púca*, it controlled attendance to the event and provided the security. For the protection of the site, the actual re-enactment and ceremony for 2019 took place some 200m to the north of the *Samhain* site, where musical entertainment, on the farm, was provided afterwards. The 2020 *Púca* Festival had to be cancelled due to COVID-19, along with many other events that have been adversely affected by the pandemic. When the fire festival will resume – and if it will be a local, small-scale event, or a corporate-sponsored touristic event – remains to be seen.

I attended the *Tlachgta* festival at Halloween for the first time in 2005 and again a few years later. On the first occasion there was storytelling from a local historian at Fair Green, after which the procession left for the hill on foot. Subsequently, the format changed slightly but always leaving from Fair Green on foot and proceeding up the hill to *Tlachtga* for the main event of the fire and the re-enactment of the *Dindshenchas Tlachtga* story.

In 2019, I participated in the festival, at the very beginning (as described in the introduction), prior to the arrival of the main participants, with the blessing of the fire and invocation of *Mogh Ruith* and an adapted invocation based on his words spoken (as documented in 'The Siege of Knocklong'). The 2019 festival was unique in that representatives of the four modern provinces and the ancient fifth province of *An Mhí* or *Míde* (Meath), arrived in separate groups, comprised of a mixture of neo-pagans – Wiccans, Druids and others. Each province was led by a woman representing a goddess and each province had its own banner. The five goddesses represented were as follows:

Meath *(Míde)*: *Éirú* (ancient goddess of sovereignty) – holding a lantern with the *Bealtaine* flame of *Uisneach*.

Leinster: *Brighid* (goddess of healing, fire, poetry and children).

Munster: *Áine* (goddess of summer, prosperity and the sun).

Connacht: *Morrígan* (also *Mór-Ríoghain*, goddess of war and prophesy).

Ulster: *Macha* (goddess of sovereignty and battle, part of the trio of goddesses *Morrígna*).

Following the arrival of the four groups, the chief Druid (druidess) gave a speech referencing the *aonach* of 1167, and called the five goddess figures to assemble and light their torches from the fire in the centre of the ringfort, before returning to their five entourages. The five provincial groups proceeded to march up the hill with the public following close behind. Unlike previous years, the procession marched past the usual *Tlachtga* entrance and entered the next field to the north, where the rest of the proceedings occurred, a short distance from the *Tlachtga* site itself.

An opening ceremony took place, involving the five goddesses, in association with the four cardinal directions plus the centre, with *Éiru* corresponding with the centre (*Míde* being the central province) and together they lit the central fire as a symbolic coming together of the entire country. McGowan subsequently explained to Michelle Alú that this unity was also representational of 'the coming together of the peoples of the world to unify in the face of challenges that we are now facing, and the changes our world is going through today'. Each of the five sovereignty goddesses were called forward one at a time to be honoured and to bestow their individual gifts and blessings on the land (country of Ireland).

McGowan explained to the public something of the relevance of *Samhain*, about the *sidhe* (fairies) and the honouring of the dead. As in previous years, a re-enactment of the story of *Tlachtga* was performed by various members of the Irish esoteric community and, as usual, it was narrated by McGowan, but with a more elaborate and extensive adaptation than had previously been undertaken.

Elements of the ceremony and re-enactment echoed earlier times and pagan gatherings at Tara. In earlier times, the provincial kings and high king (with their prominent people) would have gathered at Tara, the place of sovereignty and of ritual marriage with the land; it was here that expression of unity would have occurred primarily. In this modern age, Ireland has no high king or provincial kings, it is governed by an elected parliament. However, although there are no kings, there are Druids and other neo-pagan practitioners, such as Wiccans and Shamans, who have been able to reconvene in something akin to the ancient manner. As *Tlachtga* was the place of the Druids (while Tara was the place of royalty), perhaps it is now more appropriate that public ceremony and re-enactment should take place at *Tlachtga*.

OTHER MODERN *SAMHAIN* CELEBRATIONS

Halloween is celebrated by millions of people every October – by children in particular – as a part of modern popular culture. Over time it has transformed from a simple folk celebration into a multi-million euro/pound/dollar consumer holiday, largely divorced from its spiritual origins. Despite this rather strange commercial secularisation, it is also celebrated as *Samhain* by hundreds of thousands of neo-pagans across the world from Europe to North and South America, Australasia and Russia. In the last 100 years, or more, both Druidism and modern witchcraft (Wicca particularly) have spread across the whole world, growing in popularity, especially in the last twenty years, and so too has the celebration of the pagan New Year.

Modern *Samhain* celebrations are generally held on 31 October, but some orders, covens, groves or groups choose to celebrate at Old Halloween, sidereal Halloween/*Samhain*, which varies from year to year, falling in early November. Depending on the tradition that people follow, the forms of celebration vary. Witches and Druids tend to celebrate in different ways, as their spiritual practices and beliefs, although sometimes superficially similar, are not the same.

Adherents to the Druidic path tend to look solely to the ancient traditions of the Celtic countries for inspiration, while various forms of witchcraft may well look for inspiration from many historical sources from across Europe and beyond.

Some elements of the modern *Samhain* celebration are common to all paths, as well as to more secular celebrations. The bonfire, which appears to be universal; the reverence or remembrance of the dead is also universal, although rituals and practices will vary widely. Participation in spells, incantations and various types of divination may be practised, particularly by followers of witchcraft, although not exclusively so. Communication with spirits of the dead and with the *sidhe* may also be part of modern practices and may also include offerings of food, or in some cases a live animal, such as a chicken; again, this will vary according to the spiritual path followed. Reverence and invocation of gods/goddesses is a common practice among neo-pagans, again depending on which spiritual path is followed. Deities invoked or paid reverence to may include Irish deities linked to death or the otherworld such as the *Cailleach, Manannán Mac Lir, Donn, Crom, Morrigan* or other pagan deities such as *Hades, Persephone, Demeter, Hecate* (Greek), *Hel* and *Freya* (Norse), *Anubis, Osiris* (Egyptian), *Yama* and *Kali* (Hindu), various *Ghede, Kalfu, Legba, Maman Brigitte* (Voodoo) and many others besides.

What all of these neo-pagan festivals have in common is that they are celebrations of this time of transition rather than superstitious/secular practices based purely on fear of death, the afterlife and the unknown. Rather than being fearful of the darkness, the otherworld, the dead (ancestors) and the spirit world (*sidhe*), as is more common in the major monotheistic religions, they embrace this time of year and what it represents, as did the pre-Christian pagans of Europe.

☙❦❧

The revival of the Festival of *Samhain,* particularly at *Tlachtga* can be seen within a wider context of the revival of pagan religions during the twentieth and twenty-first centuries, in the form of neo-paganism. In particular, one can observe a renewed interest in goddess spirituality and the re-emergence of god/goddess spirituality, as an alternative to patriarchal monotheism, such as Judaism, Christianity and Islam.

As part of this trend, not only are the traditions of *Samhain*/Halloween evolving, but they are transforming and mutating as the past and the present combine, reinvigorating a tradition with roots that had been almost completely forgotten less than 100 years ago.

Bibliography

Alú, Michelle, *Tlachtga: The Samhain Festival of Fire. Layered Meanings within the Social Constructions of Sacredness and Heritage Site, and the Social Performance of Identity and Culture Belief Systems* (Maynooth University).

Archaeology Ireland, *The Hill of Ward: A Samhain site in Co. Meath* (Wordwell Ltd).

Atkinson, Robert (ed.), *Book of Ballymote* (AMS Press).

Bonwick, James, *Irish Druids and Old Irish Religions* (Sovereign Press).

Bryant, S., *Celtic Ireland* (Kegan Paul, Trench & Co.).

carrowkeel.com (website).

Duchas, 'The Schools' Collection', duchas.ie.

Eastwood, Luke, *The Druid's Primer* (Moon Books).

Eastwood, Luke, 'Tlachtga and the Ancient Roots of Halloween/Samhain', druidry.org

Frazer, James, *The Golden Bough* (Wordsworth).

Gilroy, John, *Tlachtga, Celtic Fire Festival* (Pikefield Publications).

Gwynn, Edwin (tr.), *The Metrical Dindshenchas, Part IV* (School of Celtic Studies).

Keating, G. & O'Connor, D., *Keating's General History of Ireland* (James Duffy).

Koch, John T. & Carey, John, *The Celtic Heroic Age* (Celtic Studies Publications).

labbacallee.weebly.com, 'The Murder of Mogh Ruith'.

MacAlister R.A.S. (tr.), *Lebor Gabála Érenn, Part V* (Irish Texts Society).

MacCulloch, J.A., *The Religion of the Ancient Celts* (Constable).

Mag Fhloinn, Billy, *Blood Rite: The Feast of St Martin in Ireland* (Folklore Fellows Communications).

Matthews, John (ed.), *The Druid Source Book* (Blanford).

McGarry, Tieran, 'Late pagan and Early Christian burials in Ireland: some issues and potential explanations', in Corlett, C. and Potterton, M. (eds.), *Death and Burial in Early Medieval Ireland in Light of Recent Archaeological Excavations* (Wordwell).

McGowan, Joe, *Echoes of a Savage Land* (The Mercier Press).

Meave of Connaugh, '*Tlachtga*: Revealing the Mystery', meaveofconnaugh. wordpress.com

megalithicireland.com (website).

Meyer, Kuno (Ed. and Tr.), 'The Adventures of Nera' in *Revue Celtique 10* (1889): 212–228, 520.

Meyer, Kuno (ed. and tr.), 'Corrigenda' in *Revue Celtique* 17: 319.

Moore, Caitríona, 'UCD School of Archaeology 2014:026 – *Tlachtga*, The Hill of Ward, Meath', excavations.ie

Moore, Caitríona & Davis, Stephen, 'UCD School of Archaeology 2015:171 – *Tlachtga*, The Hill of Ward, Wardstown, Meath', excavations.ie

Mullally, Erin, 'Samhain Revival: Looking for the Roots of Halloween in Ireland's Boyne Valley', *Archaeology Magazine*.

Murphy, Anthony, 'Google Imagery Reveals Fantastic Array of Drought Archaeology in Ireland', mythicalireland.com

Murphy, Anthony, 'The Cosmic Vision of Ireland's Ancient Astronomers', mythicalireland.com

Ó Catháin, Séamus, *Irish Life and Lore* (The Mercier Press).

O'Dubhain, Searles, 'Shimmering Lights and Strange Music', summerlands.com

O'Dubhain, Searles, 'The Gifts of the Gods', summerlands.com

Ó Duinn, Sean, *Where Three Streams Meet* (The Columba Press).

Ó Duinn, Sean (tr.), *Book of Lismore* (CELT).

O'Hogan Daithi, *Myth Legend & Romance* (BCA).

Ryan, Emma (ed.), *Annals of the Four Masters* (University College Cork).

Scott, Michael, *Irish Folk & Fairy Tale Omnibus* (Warner Books).

Sexton, Regina, 'Between the Realms, Food for humans, fairies and the dead at Hallowe'en', *History Ireland*, Vol. 28, No. 6.

Toland, John, *History of the Druids* (James Watt).

UCD School of Archaeology, 'The Hill of Ward Project', ucd.ie

Various, *The Anthology of Irish Folk Tales* (The History Press).

Wilmot, John, '*Samhain* Flame of *Tlachtga*', celticways.com

Wilmot, John, '*Tlachtga*, the Forgotten Goddess', celticways.com

By the Same Author

The destination for history
www.thehistorypress.co.uk

Made in the USA
Middletown, DE
21 September 2023

38855142R00082